Your Towns and Cities in

Newcastle

in the Great War

Your Towns and Cities in the Great War

Newcastle
in the Great War

Craig Armstrong

Pen & Sword
MILITARY

First published in 2015 by
Pen & Sword Military

An imprint of
Pen & Sword Books Ltd
47 Church Street
Barnsley
South Yorkshire
S70 2AS

ISBN 978 1 47382 209 2

Printed and bound in England
By CPI Group (UK) Ltd, Croydon, CR0 4YY

Pen & Sword Books Ltd incorporates the Imprints of Pen & Sword Aviation, Pen & Sword Family History, Pen & Sword Maritime, Pen & Sword Military, Pen & Sword Discovery, Pen & Sword Politics, Pen & Sword Atlas, Pen & Sword Archaeology, Wharncliffe Local History, Wharncliffe True Crime, Wharncliffe Transport, Pen & Sword Select, Pen & Sword Military Classics, Leo Cooper, The Praetorian Press, Claymore Press, Remember When, Seaforth Publishing and Frontline Publishing

For a complete list of Pen & Sword titles please contact
PEN & SWORD BOOKS LIMITED
47 Church Street, Barnsley, South Yorkshire, S70 2AS, England
E-mail: enquiries@pen-and-sword.co.uk
Website: www.pen-and-sword.co.uk

Contents

CHAPTER 1

1914
Eager for a Fight?

Pre-1914 Newcastle upon Tyne was a city built on industry and commerce which still retained a significant working class and unique character. The city had been a cradle of the Industrial Revolution and had a firm base in traditional industries such as coal mining and export, iron founding and engineering. These industries fortunes had fluctuated throughout the immediate pre-war period with coal mining moving from the city boundaries to south-east Northumberland and Durham but the Tyneside was still the main exporter of coal to British and foreign ports. The heavy-engineering industries had by and large experienced a strong and sustained period spearheaded by developments led by companies including Sir W.G. Armstrong-Whitworth and Parsons Marine Steam Turbine Company.

In tandem with these established companies there had been attempts to establish newer and more advanced industries in the city. These included the production of motor vehicles by new and established companies and the manufacturing of electrical goods. However, these attempts had not been hugely successful and, although locally important in some cases, were not to demonstrate the ability to dominate the local economy to the same extent as other more traditional industries. Even before the war, a move towards a national economy with a focus on southern England had a huge impact on several of these new companies. Joseph Swan's attempt to produce light bulbs on Tyneside between 1881 and 1886, for example, was undertaken with great local expertise and knowledge. Swan was not only a brilliant inventor, but was also a hugely successful and able businessman and he assembled a board of directors which included several high-profile entrepreneurs and businessmen (including: James Cochrane Stevenson; Theodore Merz; Hilton Philipson; and James Craig) but lasted only five years. The end came after a merger with Edison Company. The newly created Edison & Swan United Electric Light Company Limited ('Ediswan'), which was located in London, quickly came to the conclusion that it would be economically beneficial to move production away from the Tyneside and relocated their operation to Ponders End, Middlesex.

Likewise, Armstrong Whitworth attempts to enter the motor-car industry after the purchase of Wilson-Pilcher & Company a London-based car manufacturer in 1904 led to disagreements within the directors over production and research. The Wilson-Pilcher was produced at the Elswick works until 1907. After that date all vehicles produced were Armstrong Whitworth designed. Although the company was not helped by the attitude of its ageing chairman, by 1908 the production of motorcars was on a par with both Morris and Vauxhall. In 1910 and 1911, producing vehicles was actually more profitable than commercial shipbuilding. During the First World War, the company continue to produce the 17/25, 30/40 and 30/50 models and many were supplied to the military.

Although Newcastle had engineering, shipbuilding and coal exporting companies there was also a wide selection of other industrial concerns. However, some of the old industries had vanished during the immediate pre-war years. The major loss to Newcastle was the alkali trade which had declined severely until it was practically non-existent by 1900.

The concerns over the increasingly tense European situation would appear to have had a very negative effect in Newcastle as some people had focused their anger and anxiety on the small but visible German community in the city. In May 1914, the situation culminated in riots within the city which cost the ratepayers £800 for damage to property. However, these were relatively minor ripples when compared to the recent disturbances involving local suffragettes.

Although a thriving industrial centre, Newcastle upon Tyne had severe problems with poor standards of housing in many areas with poor sanitary conditions for many of the working class being commonplace. Because of the rapid growth, the city had failed to keep pace with the increasing demand for both space and new housing.[1] Although the situation had improved in the last few years, the average life expectancy in Newcastle in 1901 was just 42 years while the infant mortality rate for one year-olds in 1911 was 143 out of every 1,000. The improvement in the years leading up to the war was largely due to the good quality of shopping in the city and especially by the large numbers who were members of the Co-Operative Society. By 1905, it was estimated that 20,000 households were members and that this guarantee of quality food at a fair price was responsible for the improvement in health.[2]

As war approached the Bank Holiday weekend beckoned and many Newcastle residents, aware of the possibility of war in the near future, were determined to savour the good weather and to have an enjoyable time.

The Rush to the Colours

The North East had always had a fine military tradition and 1914 Newcastle was home to a large number of military units. The Territorial Force, which had been re-organized in 1908 along county lines, and the Northumberland Association were based at the Moot Hall, in Newcastle. The re-organization also led to a number of new drill halls being built and the Artillery Drill Hall on Barrack Road was totally rebuilt with the facilities for a riding school and the stabling for fourteen horses; training was further improved by the construction of a rifle range at Ponteland in 1914.[3]

The 1/6th (City) Battalion was based in Newcastle at St George's Drill Hall and recruited from the city and its suburbs. As part of the 50th (Northumbrian) Division the 1/6th Battalion was taking part in its annual summer camp when war broke out and it was immediately recalled and mobilized for service on 5 August. The division immediately moved to positions defending the Tyne. On 31 August, instructions were issued for all Territorial Force units to form reserve formations. This was done by assigning those men who had agreed to serve only at home to these reserve units which were bolstered by new recruits from September. The 63rd (2nd Northumbrian) Division HQ was set up at Newcastle and had responsibility for coastal defences from Seaham to Newcastle while its artillery was based at Newcastle Racecourse at Gosforth Park and its engineers at Newcastle.

To enable the Territorial Force to train effectively and to enable bases for necessary administrative duties the various units were based in local drill halls. The Barrack Road site, across from St James' Park, was home to the 1st (Northumbrian) Brigade, Royal Field Artillery, which consisted of three batteries and an ammunition column. Two of the batteries and the column were housed at Barrack Road while the 3rd Battery was housed at the Elswick Ordnance Works on Dunn Street. Upon mobilization in 1914,

Fenham Barracks, Newcastle. (Newcastle City Library)

the brigade was accommodated at the barracks and at St James' Park. The War Office paid the football club for the use of the stadium and its facilities and even housed 150 horses in makeshift stables beneath the grandstands. As previously mentioned eight companies (A through H) of the 6th (Northumberland) Battalion was based at St George's Hall, on Northumberland Road opposite the City Hall, which it shared with the Northumberland Brigade Company, Army Service Corps, which consisted of a divisional transport and supply column.

At the declaration of war, heralded by special war editions of many local newspapers, the military acted very quickly. The naval reserve was immediately called up and ordered to report to their bases. For those members of the Royal Naval Reserve (RNR) in Newcastle this meant reporting to the Mercantile Marine Office and by the end of 4 August some 250 Newcastle men had registered for service. Likewise, the men of the Territorial Force were also immediately called up and notices were posted by the city police and the army at all drill halls, police stations and in prominent places where the notices would be seen. The response was dramatic with large numbers of those men who were not on bank holiday training camps making their way immediately to their respective drill halls to report in and to find out the general situation. They were told that it was likely they would have to report for immediate duty the next morning.

Several Newcastle companies with large numbers of men in the Territorial Force reacted equally quickly to news of the war and sought to reassure the men and their families. For example, the Newcastle & Gateshead Gas Company announced just one day after the war was declared that they would pay an allowance to the wives of married workers who were called up. The company also gave an assurance that the allowance would be at least equal to that they had paid to men who had served in the Boer War and also guaranteed that any men who were called up would be re-employed at the conclusion of the war. Messrs A. Reid & Co. also agreed to pay an allowance to the dependants of their workers who were serving abroad. In this case the company was rather more generous and agreed to pay 10 shillings per week to wives and 1 shilling per week for any child of a serving employee.

On 6 August, many of the Newcastle territorial battalions left for bases in the south of England. As the men marched through the city they were applauded and cheered by large crowds and at Central Station there were large cheering crowds and emotional family scenes as loved ones said a

As a barracks town Newcastle received an influx of new recruits from all over the north. These men are from Hull and are en-route to Newcastle where they would receive initial equipment and training: Hull Daily Mail, 3 September 1914.

possibly last goodbye to fathers, sons and brothers. The platforms of the station were choked with men in khaki and the equipment of an army unit off to war. Despite the crowding the station also managed to maintain its full civilian service and the men of the territorial force were praised for the orderly nature of their departure.

The civilian response to the departure of volunteers remained extremely encouraging with huge crowds and 'tremendous scenes' as the 250 'Quaysiders' who had volunteered for service at the very start of the war left their training grounds and barracks at the Royal Grammar School and marched to Central Station to entrain for Dorset where they would form the Quayside Company of the 9th Northumberland Fusiliers. As the unit passed Barras Bridge the crowd was so dense that people could hardly move; also there were many hundreds gathered at the station to see the men depart.

Like many other areas, Newcastle witnessed an initial burst of recruitment as men joined up for a wide variety of reasons including patriotism, a desire for adventure or desperation to escape their everyday lives. The great and good of Newcastle acted quickly upon the declaration of war. On 6 August, just two days after the declaration, a meeting of influential businessmen took place at Milburn House on Dean Street; a natural choice of venue given its importance in local trade and industry (in 1907/08 it housed 185 companies). Amongst those present were Colonel W.H. Ritson, Major Robert Temperley (who was listed in the *London Gazette* as living at 11 Windsor Terrace, Newcastle), Major J. Leadbitter Knott, Mr W. J. Noble and Mr C. Cookson (a director of Cookson & Company, lead manufacturers with headquarters in Milburn House). One of the outcomes from this meeting was the formation of the Citizens Training League (in other parts of the country such units were known as Volunteer Training Corps) with Colonel Ritson as commandant; members of the league began training soon afterwards at the Royal Grammar School.

The many miners (and those engaged in mining-related work) living in Northumberland and Newcastle were very enthusiastic recruits for the 9th Battalion Northumberland Fusiliers for Lord Kitchener's 2nd Army. The battalion was formed at Newcastle in September 1914 and contained a large percentage of miners and other workers from related industries. Lord Kitchener was keen to have more battalions of the Northumberland Fusiliers formed as he held the regiment in high regard due to previous military experiences. Indeed, Newcastle led the way in recruitment and soon recruiting boards were being formed in designated areas where of men over 45 years-old would not be called up. Lord Grey and the War Office expressed the hope that other districts would follow the example set by Newcastle and various Northumberland communities. The response of the miners was phenomenal; by December it was believed that of the 170,000 in the Northumberland and Durham coalfields almost 25 per cent had joined up (over 40,000) and that the north-easterners, including men from Newcastle, made ideal recruits as they were already hard and disciplined. Recruitment continued to be strong and further meetings were held across the region including in Newcastle. However, there was some resentment when it was alleged that the wives of those who had joined up would be observed by the police; presumably in reaction to the fear of declining moral standards amongst those women left behind.

However, even this development could not keep pace with the surge to volunteer. A meeting of the Council of the Newcastle & Gateshead Chamber of Commerce was called on 2 September to discuss the possible raising of a battalion of infantry for the Northumberland Fusiliers. This meeting was addressed by Mr George Renwick, MP, who called for the chamber to assist with this and urged them to ask the Mayor, Colonel Johnstone Wallace, to agree to the raising of such a force. Major Temperley replied that he believed that the chamber could best help by appealing to those classes of young men with whom it was associated and that the chamber offer to 'raise, organize and equip a battalion of infantry from amongst the younger commercial men on the Quayside and "up-street".'

As seemed to be common practice the War Office response to the offer to recruit a battalion met with a lacklustre response and several days went by with no reply. However, the news had leaked out locally and there was an overwhelming response with over 400 men volunteering. On 7 September, a full company (250 men), impatient to be getting on with things, agreed to accept enlistment in the 9th (Service) Battalion and left Newcastle bound for the training depot in Dorset.[4]

This eagerness to join up was bolstered by the eagerness of some to form what later became known as 'Pals Battalions'. It was believed, correctly, that men were more likely to join up in the knowledge that they would be fighting alongside men they knew or who at least shared similar backgrounds or jobs. Indeed, the proposal to raise a battalion from the Chamber of Commerce claimed that one of attractions of the proposal was that "comrades would be enabled to serve side by side".[5] It is claimed that the 16th (Newcastle) Battalion of the Northumberland Fusiliers was the first to be raised in the

Men of the Tyneside Commercials Battalion, without even a basic uniform as yet, on a practice route march: Illustrated Chronicle, 12 September 1914.

north of England by civilian effort. Remarkably, and demonstrating the initial burst of enthusiasm, the battalion was raised in the course of just eight days (8 to 16 September). Colonel Ritson was appointed commanding officer; a task for which he was eminently qualified as he had a long history of service including being the first commander of the 6th (Territorial) Northumberland Fusiliers in 1908.

After initial formation in September 1914 and training throughout 1915 at locations in Shropshire and Yorkshire the battalion was posted to France, landing at Boulogne on the 22 November 1915. The 'Tyneside Commercials', as they became widely known, saw heavy action throughout the war including at the Somme in 1916, the Ancre and the German army's retreat to the Hindenburg Line in 1917. In the final year of the war the battalion saw action on the Somme again, the Battle of the Hindenburg Line and in the final 100 days advance in Picardy.

The general enthusiasm for joining up to serve with friends was very strong in Newcastle, as it was elsewhere, and men often chose to join units organized around specific trades, areas, activities and national backgrounds. On 12 September, the *Newcastle Evening Chronicle* featured a letter to the editor suggesting the formation of a new regiment of 'Tyneside Irish'. The letter was signed by several influential men with links to the Irish community including the Mayor of Wallsend, councillors, a Justice of the Peace, the president and secretary of the Irish National Club and the secretary of the Ancient Order of Hibernians (England). This new regiment would recruit from the very large numbers of Irishmen and those of Irish descent. Although the relationships between the Irish and non-Irish community had at times been strained (there were tensions within the community along political and religious lines) the appeal was for men of all denominations and classes to serve alongside one another. To further develop the idea, a meeting was arranged to take place at the Irish National Club at Collingwood Hall in Clayton Street on the next day (Sunday, 13 September). The letter asked for 'every representative Irishman on Tyneside, regardless of politics or religion,'[6] should consider it his duty to go to the meeting.

Initially the plan was for the unit to offer its services to the 16th (Irish) Division which was then being formed in Eire. Disgracefully the offer was very impolitely rebuffed by the commander of the 16th Division who claimed that the men being raised in the north east were 'slum birds'.[7] On 18 September, a further blow befell the organizers when the War Office declined the offer of a battalion of 'Tyneside Irish' claiming that a sufficient number of local battalions were already being organized. It was through that this rebuff came as a result of the row between the War Office and the committee which was raising the 'Tyneside Scottish'.

For the time being this put an end to the recruitment of the 'Tyneside Irish' and many of the men who had offered to join were instead recruited into other formations, including the 'Tyneside Scottish'. In early October, Lord Haldane visited Newcastle to deliver a request from Lord Kitchener for the recruitment of a battalion of 'Tyneside Scottish' and the Lord Mayor of Newcastle was recognized as the raiser of the 'Tyneside Brigades'. This event gave new hope to the many within the Irish community that a similar unit of 'Tyneside Irish' would now be authorized. A subsequent request from the War Office for the recruitment of a 'Tyneside Brigade' made up of 'Tyneside Scottish, Irish' and a further 'Commercials Battalion'. The recruitment centre for this new formation was the Corn Exchange and recruitment proceeded apace for the Scottish but for the Irish was much slower, probably as a result of the previous disappointment and the fact that many men had joined other units as a result. There is some debate over who the first official 'Tyneside Irish' recruit was as the *Newcastle Evening Chronicle* claimed that they were Patrick Butler of Newcastle (who was killed as a sergeant on the first day of the Somme) and James Leach of Hebburn while the historian Joseph Keating claims that it was in fact the son of one of the committee, Henry Doyle.

The men who joined the 'Tyneside Irish' reflected the Newcastle community and included many who had previously served in the army (most of these later formed the basis of a valuable experienced cadre of NCOs), men who had been born in Ireland and those of Irish parentage and a number whose only connection with Ireland was that they attended a church with strong Irish links or worked with an Irishman. Many were said to be illiterate and standards of clothing and cleanliness were often poor. One of the officers of the new unit claimed that many of the men had been influenced to sign up because they were poor and malnourished. It is a key point that to many of the working classes in Newcastle, service in the army during wartime offered risks, which were seen as being, no more deadly than their pre-war lives had offered while there were some benefits such as clothing being provided along with regular food. In common with the majority of newly-raised 'pals' battalions the enthusiasm to volunteer had outpaced officialdom and the men at first had no uniforms but instead the three Tyneside battalions wore different colours to denote their unit (a green armband for the Irish, a red lanyard for the commercials and a Royal Stewart tartan armband for the Scots).

One of the greatest difficulties faced in the raising of the volunteer battalions in Newcastle was funding the effort. Eventually the War Office would take over responsibility but initially the burden was to be born by the raising committees. Once again, local initiatives and gifts by the wealthy and enthusiastic solved many of the problems with Joseph Cowen being especially generous in giving £10,000 to cover costs of raising volunteer units until the government took over.

Men of the Tyneside Commercials practice their 'War Dance' (presumably during exercise) on the Town Moor: Newcastle Chronicle, October 1914.

With the financial costs now covered the organization of the necessary recruitment policies proceeded quickly. As was normal it was the great and good of Newcastle who led the way, backed by representatives of various churches such as the Dean of St Mary's Roman Catholic Cathedral and Reverend C.E. Osborne representing the Church of England. This meeting agreed that the first meeting of the executive committee for the 'Tyneside Irish' was to be held on 21 October. Just three days after this first meeting the recruitment campaign swung into action with recruitment posters appearing in local newspapers urging 'Irishmen to Arms!' while other posters in the green and gold of Ireland appeared across the city. The initial effect was encouraging with over 300 men signing up in the first week. The recruitment campaign continued with meetings, speeches and further posters and by the end of October a commanding officer had been appointed and two fields for training, behind Jesmond Gardens, had been offered by Colonel Ritson. Each poster had a form which men could sign and post to the committee and fifteen recruitment offices were opened across the north east with three being in Newcastle (at the Town hall, the Corn Exchange and at 57 Westgate Road). Morning parades of the new unit were held in Eldon Square at 9.00am. Even at this stage many of the men did not have weapons and the site of the men marching off to begin a days training led by the instantly recognizable Major Joe Prior was a somewhat incongruous sight. Uniquely the 'Tyneside Irish' committee also placed advertisements for officers and NCOs.

Recruitment boards could also rely on influential visitors to recruitment meetings and on 10 October two meetings were held simultaneously in Newcastle at the Tyne and Pavilion Theatres. Both meetings were visited by guest speaker in the form of Lord Curzon (who later served in the war cabinets of Asquith and Lloyd George), Lord Haldane (at the time Lord Chancellor before he was hounded out of office in 1915 by a *Daily Mail* campaign claiming he had pro-German leanings) and Mr Arthur Henderson, MP (member of parliament for Barnard Castle and leader of the Labour Party).

Other efforts at recruitment had a more sinister side. At the instigation of the managing editor of the *Newcastle Chronicle*, Colonel Joseph Reed, the details and addresses of those who had volunteered were published in the newspapers. The aim of this measure was to shame those who had not offered their services.

By the start of November, the battalion was at half strength and there were problems arising over the accommodation of the men (many of whom were from outside Newcastle). The problem was again solved by Joseph Cowen

Soldiers receiving gifts in Newcastle.

Pupils and teacher (Miss Phyllis) from Bolam Street School, Byker, c.1915.
(Newcastle City Library)

Many Newcastle schools set up Officer Training Corps and Cadet Corps during the war. This is Dame Allan's School's Cadet Corps, c.1914.

East Walker School, 1914-1918. The war for many of Newcastle's children meant separation from fathers and brothers and an increasingly poor diet. How many of these young lads lost a father or brother one wonders? (Newcastle City Library)

who offered another £5,000 to defray the costs of accommodation and to fund the purchase of Dunn's Buildings at Low Friar Street. It was estimated that this building could house up to 800 men in comfort. In addition to this, 200 men were initially housed in the Town Hall before being moved to the vacant Raby Street School.

Recruitment was maintained throughout November when the 'Tyneside Irish' committee formed a ladies committee in order to facilitate the provision of the volunteers with some home comforts. The first activity of this ladies committee was to make an urgent appeal for warm overcoats and for money to buy warm clothing. This campaign was buoyed on by the names of those who contributed being published in local newspapers. Donations of time, money and other resources from local businesses and worthies continued to aid the recruitment and training effort with, for example, Messrs George & Jopling donating the use of a motor car to the committee. By 4 November, the 'Tyneside Irish' battalion was at full strength with men to spare. The ages of the Irish recruits was a cause for concern with the average being men in their late thirties and a number over 40 years-old. At the other end of the spectrum there was also the usual number of underage boys who wished to join up and had slipped through the recruiting net; in the case of the Irish there were at least two in Private Arthur Walton who was 14 years-old and Private Edward Armstrong who was a year older. The unit's first Regimental Sergeant Major (P. O'Toole) was unable to serve abroad due to his age and was discharged in 1916 as he was 60 years-old. Like many Newcastle residents he was not left untouched by the war as his son John J. O'Toole was killed while serving as a sergeant in the 1st Battalion Irish Guards on the same day that the 'Tyneside Irish' was declared to be at full strength.

By early November, it had become clear that the numbers of those willing to volunteer was outpacing the current demands of the War Office and the recruitment committees began to entertain thoughts of a more ambitious nature. By the second week in November, the committee of the 'Tyneside Irish' began to consider the formation of a second battalion as the numbers of volunteers continued to be high although the first battalion was now at full strength. Petitions to the War Office for permission to form a second battalion were successful and, as recruitment had been ongoing, this battalion was at full strength within two days of the news being received. The committee then began considering the formation of a third battalion (permission was granted on 23 November). Recruitment continued to be healthy throughout December with a small lull over the Christmas period but the numbers increased again immediately after the holiday period and this encouraged the committee to make arrangements for a fourth battalion which would complete a 'Tyneside Irish Brigade'. Although many of the recruits came from outside Newcastle there were a large number of Newcastle natives within the ranks and all of the recruitment organization and billeting was performed in the city.

Demonstrating the enthusiastic response that was present in Newcastle eighteen battalions of Northumberland Fusiliers were raised in Newcastle between August and December 1914. At the outbreak of the war the strength of a British infantry battalion was 1,107 men commanded by a lieutenant colonel, thus almost 20,000 men must have volunteered for service with the regiment during these five months. The city was justifiably proud of its record in voluntarism and as early as the beginning of September it was being reported in the national press that Newcastle held the record for recruiting and that over 10,000 men had already volunteered; a huge number for Newcastle's size. Northumberland Fusilier battalions formed in Newcastle during 1914 included the following:

August: 8th (Service).

September: 9th (Service), 10th (Service), 11th (Service), 12th (Service), 13th (Service), 14th (Service), 21st (Service) (2nd 'Tyneside Scottish').

October: 18th (Service) (1st Tyneside Pioneers), 20th (Service) (1st 'Tyneside Scottish').

November: 19th (Service) (2nd Tyneside Pioneers), 22nd and 23rd (Service) (3rd and 4th 'Tyneside Scottish'), 24th, 25th and 26th (Service) (1st, 2nd and 3rd 'Tyneside Irish').

December: 2/6th (Territorial).

The author of the official history of the 16th Battalion, Northumberland Fusiliers, claimed that in Newcastle the rush to the colours was phenomenal with the bureaucracy unable to keep up with the numbers of volunteers. The procedure of formal attestations quickly fell behind due to the surge of potential volunteers.

Training of the volunteer units was another problem and was overcome, at least by the 16th battalion, by giving anyone with previous military experience command of twenty to thirty men. Drill grounds were organized on an informal basis with school fields (such as those at the Royal Grammar School) and the Town Moor being used as temporary parade and training grounds. The school contributed in other ways too with the members of its Officer Training Corps assisting in the training of new recruits and with many of it former pupils volunteering for service. In common with most other parts of the country the volunteers initially lacked uniforms and instead had to settle for the blue-grey (and deeply unpopular, though hardwearing) uniform produced by Bainbridge & Co. So unpopular was this uniform that the 'Tyneside Irish' instead commissioned their own uniforms in the more traditional khaki as they believed that this would attract more recruits from among those who objected to wearing what had become known as 'Kitchener Blue' uniforms.

Despite the problems it appears that the populace of Newcastle were justifiably proud of 'their' battalions and route marches and parades were usually met by supportive crowds. This was the case in mid-September when the 1/6th (City) Territorial Battalion of the Northumberland Fusiliers, whose base was at St George's Drill Hall, and elements of the 16th battalion paraded in front of the Town Hall. Battalions made great use of such opportunities to encourage further recruitment with a church parade held by the 16th at the cathedral in October being particularly encouraging. The Christmas parade held on 23 December by the first battalion of the 'Tyneside Irish' in Eldon Square was very warmly received with a large crowd and positive newspaper coverage. To maintain morale a concert and large Christmas dinner with beer was provided for the men of the battalion.

As November wore on, however, there was grumbling as the papers, and popular opinion, still held that the war would be of short duration and many men, anxious for action, became disgruntled because they wanted to 'do more' before the war ended. In this atmosphere rumours began to take hold and when a mysterious call for volunteers who had experience of musketry went out and such men were told they must be ready for any emergency at a moments notice the rumour quickly went about that a large German invasion force was preparing to land on the north east coast. These men were formed into what became known as the 'Composite Battalion', which was intended to defend the north east coast, and for the first night were billeted at the grammar school before being moved to Clarence Street schools which were cramped and dirty. While no invasion occurred the men of the composite battalion were kept locked up, without passes in their hated new billet; resentment grew. At the conclusion of this pointless episode, three weeks later, the men were relieved when they were order to report back to their parent units.

It became clear that the men of the new service battalions would benefit from exposure to regular camp life as it was thought that men training and

The shipyards of Tyneside produced incredible amounts of shipping during the war. Although this is across the Tyne at Jarrow it gives some idea of the work on the river. (Newcastle City Library)

The Tyne was also a vital port and the shipyards and docks remained manically busy throughout the war. (Newcastle City Library)

The Mauritania *sailing from the Tyne. The shipyards were not only famed for their naval vessels but also for their merchants and liners. The* Mauritania *at the time was the fastest ship in the world (a record she held until 1929). She served as a troopship and a hospitalship during the war.* (Newcastle City Library)

HMS Superb *on the Tyne.* (Newcastle City Library)

HMS Invincible *being launched at Elswick in 1907. The ship is without her armament and would be destroyed at Jutland with most of her crew.* (Newcastle City Library)

HMS Monarch *under steam on the Tyne.* (Newcastle City Library)

then returning home at night was holding back the development of the units. Training was also being restricted by the problems of being based in the city. One thing that was practiced was the digging and maintaining of trenches on a specially selected area of the Town Moor. The 'Tyneside Irish' were said to be particularly adept at this skill due to the large number of miners within its ranks. Thus the majority of battalions were quickly posted to camps outside of the city as soon as basic training was completed with many, including the 16th, being sent to the newly constructed camp in the park of the Duke of Northumberland's estate at Alnwick.

As a mercantile port city the people of Newcastle, of course, had a strong tradition of service at sea; in both naval and mercantile services. The shore-based establishment HMS *Calliope* on the Tyne was home to the Royal Naval

The port of Newcastle was exceptionally busy as this 1909 picture shows. During the war the docks were even busier with essential cargoes. (Newcastle City Library)

Volunteer Reserve (RNVR) and also the army, which both recruiting heavily in Newcastle. Indeed, the response was so great that the Royal Navy also formed a body of infantry as it was recruiting too many men. The commanding officer in Newcastle, Lieutenant Commander H.J. Craig, RNVR, MP, was able to state that his unit was sending 200 recruits a week for service with the Naval Division and that the city had already provided 1,100 men for the division which was assembling at The Crystal Palace in London.

The naval bombardment of east coast towns had another effect in that it was felt that the attack might convince those who were perceived as slacking and avoiding joining up to revise their opinions in view of the enemy's willingness to bombard civilian population centres. After the bombardment there was a series of cartoons and editorials which encouraged those 'slackers' to enlist in order to fight those who had killed the innocent. Indeed there was an increase in volunteering after the bombardment and it seems that the act and the subsequent propaganda campaign did play a role in determining some young men to volunteer.

Other recruits who passed through Newcastle in 1914 were neither British nor bound for service in the British army or navy. In October, a group of 117 Canadian-Russians arrived in the city. The men, who were all artisans, had agreed to serve in their mother country's forces and were en-route to Petrograd. It was said that the men all possessed fine physiques and that they were cheerful despite the hardships of their journey.

Business as Usual?

With the advent of war the trade associations of Newcastle quickly met in order to vow their support in the crisis, but also to put in place plans for emergencies and to discuss how the war would affect trade. Within a port city the prime concern for many was how they could manage to maintain the supply of goods and materials during wartime. The Newcastle, Gateshead & District Grocers & Provisions Dealers held a very well attended emergency meeting at the Collingwood Restaurant in the Groat Market. At the meeting it quickly became clear that many were extremely concerned as it meant that increasing food prices (particularly flour) would mean that grocers might be unable to restock their shops. The concerns expressed over the prices being asked for flour demonstrated the anger of many members of the group. Members commented that the price of flour had, 'gone up tremendously, and it was continuing to rise at a very rapid rate', while Mr A. Taylor added that he believed the public were making matters worse by panic buying before showing some naivety as to the national situation by mistakenly commenting that there was 'any amount of wheat in the country'. The flour prices were a very serious cause for anxiety and, indeed, alarm as it was explained that prices had again increased and the Newcastle Exchange reported that the price of finest flour had increased by 11 shillings, super by 12 shillings and patent by 10 shillings.[8] Mr J.W. Robinson spoke on behalf of many members when he stated, 'none of them wished to make as much profit as possible. They wanted to sell at a fair profit'. Concerns were also voiced over the amount of butter that was available and it was widely believed that if price rises continued in the manner they were then the supply of Danish butter in Newcastle would be exhausted within the week. Clearly these men did have valid concerns but it is also clear that they did remain determined to pass costs onto the customer in order to make their own businesses much more profitable and that they largely blamed the general public for the shortage of goods. This was very clearly demonstrated as the meeting concluded by voting on a motion that prices should be raised in line with supply costs and that the public be urged to remain calm and buy as usual.

However, the impact of the war on the usual commercial activities of Newcastle and Tyneside became clear as early as 5 August when the *Newcastle Daily Chronicle* reported that only half the usual number of herring drifters had arrived in the Tyne and that the trade would therefore be depressed. Worries over supplies continued for the first weeks of the war with the supply of continental yeast being completely cut off but the British manufacturers responded by issuing declarations that given a few weeks they would be able to cover the lost imports themselves as long as the government did not purchase necessary supplies of wheat and/or oats for other uses. On the plus side the summer had seen the most productive potato crop for many years and the fruit crop was also looking extremely promising.

The lack of supplies combined with panic buying and the high prices being charged by suppliers resulted in the closure of a large number of Newcastle shops. The closure of these shops and their refusal to accept orders from customers was reported to have caused 'anxiety and excitement' amongst the women of the city who were responsible for keeping the home supplied. One leading firm in Blackett Street was even forced to close due to lack of supplies and a member of staff had to face an angry and clamouring crowd of women to explain that they were completely sold out. It was reported that for most shops there was no flour, no sugar and that eggs could not be

Damage to the funnel of the SS Isle of Hastings, *a Newcastle based steamer which was heading back to Britain. She was damaged while at Philippeville in Algeria: Hull Daily Mail, 9 September 1914.*

purchased for 'love nor money', while the price of bacon had doubled to 2 pence per lb.[9]

When war was declared there were a number of German registered ships in British ports and in British waters. On 6 August, more than twenty vessels representing 40,000-tons of shipping had been seized. At Newcastle the German-owned *Henry Furst*, a steamer of almost 1,500-tons was seized. The ship was berthed at Dunston from where it was to depart for Russia with a cargo of coal. A court writ proclaiming the vessel officially as a prize was made in the High Court of Justice and was published in *The Times* on 29 August.

As one of the cornerstones of British industry, Newcastle was to play a vitally important role in the national war effort. The prevalence of key industries such as shipbuilding, marine engineering, armaments and heavy engineering combined with the city's importance as a port (particularly transporting coal) resulted in Tyneside being essential to the production and distribution of vital war material. Those sailing in and out of the Tyne placed their lives at risk all the time they were at sea with threats from submarines, naval units and mines. Many vessels were lost such as the steamer SS *Leersum* of Amsterdam which was sunk (along with another unknown steamer which it had stopped to help) after striking a mine while en-route from Rotterdam to Newcastle with what was described as a general cargo. Two of the crew were lost; a Dutch sailor and a Belgian refugee who had signed on as a fireman.

In an industrial sense, Newcastle possessed a small variety of key industries which dominated but also a large number of smaller firms producing a wide range of products and although this was to prove important to the war effort it did result in a narrow focus which, it has been argued, limited expansion into other, newer, and more profitable areas of production.

Even the smaller engineering companies in Newcastle played vital roles as the war went on; George & Jobling Motor Engineers (located at the old Stephenson Works on Forth Banks), for example, had an interest in both motor vehicles and also aircraft design and production. The company had taken over the site (made famous by George and Robert Stephenson) and specialized in fitting their own bodywork on Ford and Argyll motor-car chassis and also built bodywork for other vehicles. The companies' interest in pioneering aviation was a result of Arthur Edward George (1875-1951). A remarkable man, George had been an international-class swimmer, figure skater, cyclist and a highly-successful racing-car driver before he developed an interest in aviation. George took lessons and in 1910 was awarded pilot's license No 19 from the Royal Aero Club before returning to his business interests where he helped to invent the forerunner of the trolley jack and his own bi-plane aircraft. The machine he had designed featured some unique innovations and he wished to put it into full production but, following a crash, the banks refused to give him funding on the grounds that the venture was too risky and he was forced to abandon the idea. Throughout the war, the factory produced a variety of items including transport for the armed forces; A.E. George also served as a major in the Northumberland Motor Volunteer Corps.

Given the importance of the coal trade to Newcastle it was worrying that in the first weeks of the war the trade declined as buyers were concerned primarily with the delivery of orders already placed. On 13 August, the midweek market at Newcastle was described as being nominal. Initial worries over the vulnerability of shipping lanes off the east coast caused some disruption as some companies diverted their ships to what were seen as more secure ports. On 16 August, the United Steamship Company of Copenhagen ordered its steamers to divert from Newcastle to the port of Leith.

The outbreak of war had an initially devastating effect on the vitally important coal export trade upon which so many Newcastle businesses depended. Just one day after the declaration the Newcastle Exchange was reporting that the trade was very depressed and that if the situation continued

Newburn, Spencer's Steel Works, taken just after the end of the war. (Newcastle City Library)

much longer many pits would be forced to close due to the lack of demand. Of course this did not only affect miners but also the dock workers, collier crews, coal merchants and ship owners.[10] On 6 August, it was reported that 50,000 northern colliers were idle and that if the situation continued many miners, shipyard workers and stevedores would lose their jobs. This further encouraged a large number of these men to enrol in the armed forces and further swelled the rush to the colours.

As an industrial hub Newcastle possessed many industries of great importance to the war effort. The *Kelly's Directory* of 1914 lists the most important industries as being: shipbuilding, the production of locomotives and marine engines, bridge works, steam engines and machinery, heavy ordnance, private carriages and harness; lead smelting and refining, the manufacture of a number of varieties of lead and shot; glass and earthenware manufacture; chemical manures, alkalis, cement, brick and tile manufacturers, firebricks; tar, coke, turpentine, colours, iron castings, wrought iron, steel and brass; production of files, nails, shovels and other tools; paper production; malting; grindstones and millstones; hemp and wire manufacture, rope and sail-making, cable and anchor production; tanning and shoe manufacturing. All of these industries would play roles in the war effort and many of the companies could also turn their hands to other things.

Because of the number of industries that would be of vital importance in the national war effort Newcastle did not suffer from the high unemployment that was commonplace in other northern areas. A special correspondent in *The Times* described the city as being 'an oasis in the desert of distress.'[11] Unemployment in the city was lower than in 1912 and huge number of government orders had created a mini boom in several industries; most notably shipbuilding and armaments. At this early stage in the war, Sir W.G. Armstrong Whitworth & Co., Palmer's, Hawthorn Leslie & Swan, Hunter & Wigham Richardson were employing tens of thousands of men and were operating constantly around the clock.

In terms of the military war effort, the most important Newcastle-based industry was the production of armaments and in Newcastle that largely meant Sir W.G. Armstrong Whitworth & Co. The company, which had been the brainchild of Lord Armstrong, produced guns, shells, ships and other equipment vital to the national war effort. The main site at Elswick extended for over a mile along the river bank and had an area of 72 acres and in 1914 the company employed approximately 25,000 men. Elswick functioned as an ordnance factory, steelworks and shipyard producing fully-armed naval vessels. The company also had a shipyard at Walker which produced merchant vessels, a site at Scotswood which produced motorcars and wagons, and a second site in Walker which operated as a fitting-out yard. Armstrong-Whitworth also operated factories at Openshaw, Manchester and at Pozzuoli in Italy. The rush of wartime order and the ongoing need for supplies meant that Armstrong's underwent massive growth during the war. (see Chapter 5)

The rush to enlist described earlier in this chapter had a severe knock-on effect on vital war industries in Newcastle with severe labour shortages affecting most firms. As early as September, Armstrong Whitworth had lost almost 10 per cent of its workforce with almost 2,000 men enlisting; while Hawthorn-Leslie & Swan had lost nearly 1,000.[12] Other companies offered the services of their workers by placing advertisements in national newspapers. These included the Yost Typewriter Co. Ltd which, among other locations, had offices at 114 Pilgrim Street. On Friday, 7 August, the company placed an advertisement in the *The Times* offering the services of 100 experienced typists and short-hand writers for immediate government service at any location.[13]

Newcastle also played a role as an important national transport hub. The city was on a main-railway line linking Scotland and England and

Newcastle with Carlisle on the west coast. The city had a large and impressive goods station at Forth Banks which spread across 4½ acres and contained extensive underground warehouse cellars and the old New Bridge Street station had been converted into mineral sidings. In addition to this warehousing capacity, a large new facility at New Bridge Street had also been recently built.

As the Northumberland and Durham coalfields produced a quarter of all coal in Great Britain (34,514,835t in 1912) and much of this was transported by the North Eastern Railway with its main base at Central station on Neville Street. The Tyne was one of the three most important ports in Britain for the shipping of coal (the other two being the Wear and the Tees) and two years before the war had been responsible for the shipping of almost 2,500,000t of coal around the British coast and exported almost 6,500,000t. Although the coal industry was important there were, by the start of the war, only a handful of collieries left within the city boundaries. These collieries supplied the local demand and were little affected by the slump in international trade which had so badly affected exports from Northumberland.

The declining coal-export trade led to temptation on the part of at least one Newcastle businessman and ended in a charge of trading with the enemy. Mr Thomas Hartley Seed, managing director of Messrs Harper, Seed & Company coal exporters, was charged with having attempted to trade with the enemy. It was alleged that he had tried to trade with an American firm, the Gans Steamship Company, which had an office in Hamburg and which sailed into German ports. Mr Seed had written in a letter, which was intercepted, to Mr Carl Wohlenburg at Aarhus declaring that he would be happy to continue trading and also because of the 'patriotic mood' in the industry locally (which had resulted in mines seeking to continue to employ miners despite lack of demand) it might be possible 'squeeze some of them' into even lower prices. Mr Seed's defence declared that the coal was to be supplied to the United States and that Mr Wohlenburg was a German agent of a New York company.[14]

A further hearing saw Mr Seed have other charges directed against him. The Crown alleged that Mr Seed, in conjunction with another director, Frederick Petersen (a naturalized German who lived in London), had traded with the enemy, conspired in the creation of felicitous documents, making false entries in company registers, conspiracy to contravene the provisions of the Companies Act and of possessing forged certificates. The prosecutor declared that Harper, Seed & Co. consisted of four shareholding directors: Mr Seed, Mr Petersen and two German brothers named Horn who lived at Lubeck and Schelswig. It was further alleged that at the outbreak of war Mr Seed had written to the two Germans suggesting that their shares be transferred to himself and Petersen as it was possible that German interests would be commandeered by the government. The two were remanded in custody for committal at the assizes with bail being set at £500 with sureties of £250 each.

The case came before the assizes on 6 November, where Mr Seed and Mr Petersen both pleaded guilty to attempting to trade with the enemy. Both defendants were facing a variety of charges surrounding their attempt to make bogus transfers of shares from their German partners. Mr Justice Shearman, presiding, fined Mr Seed the sum of £100 and Mr Petersen £50. He declared that he was satisfied that there had been no attempt to make payments to German citizens and that Mr Seed had acted from a misplaced and possibly generous impulse to protect the investment of his German partners. *The Times* seemed to take a dim view of the sentencing as a similar charge against an Edinburgh-based businessman, Mr William Drummond Dick, heard on the same day resulted in a five year penal servitude sentence.

Other companies looked to the patriotic fervour as a source of possible revenue by offering products which would be suitable as gifts to soldiers at the front or to hospitals. One such was IDL Industrials Limited of Pilgrim Street, who placed adverts in the national press promoting their 20 shilling parcels of patented IDL surgical bandages which it claimed were the 'Last Word' in scientific production and which were stronger and more absorbent than other bandages but for less cost. It stated that the offer of these parcels was a unique one and that the bandages would be 'suitable for Gifts to Ambulance Corps, etc.'. [15]

While the industries of wartime importance boomed there were worries over several other trades. The building trades, for example, were very subdued and many men, from skilled craftsmen to building labourers, were threatened with unemployment. This was despite the large numbers of men who were volunteering for service at the time. The City Council was proactive in this matter as it recognized the importance of retaining many of these men within the labour force. It was therefore agreed that the council would enter into contracts to the value of £70,000 for work in the city.

The shipyard workers found themselves stretched during the first year of the war and round-the-clock working shifts were put in place. Aware of the importance of the industries in Newcastle the government, local authorities and the King all made efforts to reassure the workers that they were aware of their contribution and efforts. In December, a visit by Dr Macnamara on behalf of the Board of the Admiralty praised the workers and compared them to the men serving in the navy and in the trenches while acknowledging that, 'great and continuous strain had been put upon them…and they had responded patriotically.'[16] The Lord Mayor of Newcastle telegraphed a thank you to the King and received a reply stating, 'The King appreciates the loyal and untiring service which is being rendered to the country by the skilled workmen in the great ship-building and armaments firms. His Majesty greatly admires the spirit of patriotism… by work they alone can most successfully perform they are assisting in the prosecution of the war equally with their comrades serving by land and sea.'[17]

Much of the heavy industrial work on Tyneside was almost as dangerous as serving in the military and there were relatively frequent accidents and even fatalities. One such was the case of Mr William Harrison who worked at Elswick Shipyard and was killed in an accident there while working on a Norwegian battleship, the *Nidaros*.[18] In the course of the war, a large number of Newcastle men lost their lives due to industrial accidents and these men, and their families, received little recognition for the sacrifices that they had also made in the national war effort.

A People's War?

The people of Newcastle appear to have accepted the declaration of war and the initial changes to their routine with magnanimity and it was reported that the population was calm with no shouting or overly passionate feelings to be heard and that, contrary to common belief, the majority believed that the war would be a long one and that they were treating it with the utmost seriousness. As the war was declared during a public holiday period many Newcastle residents were at the seaside at Whitely Bay and Tynemouth but many, accepting that this might represent the last opportunity to enjoy the sunshine and relax for some time had remained there rather than returning home panic-stricken. Indeed, *The Times* reporter stated on 15 August, 'sands at Whitley Bay to-day were crowded with children, bathers and a cheerful holiday throng.'[19] In the city of Newcastle, the Theatre Royal was proud to advertise Mr Martin Harvey in several plays including, *The Taming of the Shrew*, *Hamlet* and *The Breed of the Treshams*. [20] Ironically, this last is a play concerned the activities of a roundhead spy during the siege of Faversham and its popularity can be partially attributed to the growing spy fever.

The bank holiday weekend of August saw fine weather and, despite the gathering war clouds, the people of Newcastle were generally cheerful. Although the war had cast a sobering shadow over many people it is clear from contemporary accounts that the majority of Newcastle residents remained determined to enjoy the bank holiday weekend and to make the most of the good weather. Many had journeyed to Tynemouth and Whitley Bay in order to enjoy the seaside while others had set off on bicycles to explore the Northumberland countryside. A large number had journeyed by train or bicycle to Hexham to attend the annual Tyneside Agricultural Society Show on Bank Holiday Monday. Clearly the vast majority were perfectly willing to continue with their normal lives as the crowd was estimated at over 10,000. Many others enjoyed more raucous pursuits; the theatres, music halls and picture halls were all well attended. The majority of venues hosted their advertised shows but many added a patriotic flavour with the packed audience at the Empire standing for the national anthem before the show began. It was reported that the audience thoroughly enjoyed the acts with Maidie Scott proving an especial hit with a new character study entitled *Troubles of a Stage-Struck Girl*.[21]

The formal declaration of war was met with a variety of responses. Many people still believed that the war would be over quickly and that it was a matter for the army and would not have a wide-reaching effect on society as a whole. Others, encouraged by much of the local press coverage, believed that the war was just and that it would be an opportunity once more for Britain to show its superiority and to put Germany in its place. Others, however, realized that the war was likely to be long, arduous and extremely costly and reacted with a sense of resigned dread. Still others, especially amongst the Wesleyan Methodist community, were appalled and reacted by strongly denouncing the war and held meetings and rallies to demand that Britain remain neutral. The Methodist churches continued to protest loudly over the course of the next few days and weeks.

Morale generally seems to have been very well maintained during the first few months of war with the majority of people generally making the best of the situation (though they quickly grew angry at the thought of profiteering and suspicions of enemy aliens remained high) and patriotically supporting the war effort. Humour was said to be good and small comic incidents were reported in the local newspapers. One example was a conversation overheard in a Newcastle cafe during which a customer asked, 'have you any Berlin buns?' only to be told by the waitress, 'no ma'am. Only Belgian buns now'.[22]

The local press reacted to the news of the formal declaration in a generally balanced manner with a great deal of analysis of the situation, especially the dangers to the North-East coast if Germany captured the ports of the

HMS Monarch *sailing below the Tyne bridges in 1911.* (Newcastle City Library)

Low Countries. The balanced nature of the reporting was mixed with the usual local news and advertisements but also with patriotic sentiment and encouragements for everyone to do their bit. In order to bolster morale and to reflect public pride the local press ran stories extolling the contribution made to the armed forces by Newcastle based industries. On just the third day of the war, and reflecting the pride in the local shipbuilding industry, the *Newcastle Weekly Chronicle* ran a story praising the shipyard workers and listing several of the warships that had been built on the Tyne and were now protecting Britain by serving in the Grand Fleet at Scapa Flow. These included HMS *Superb* (built by Armstrong Whitworth, the fourth ever dreadnought, a 22,000-ton Bellerephon-class battleship which survived the Battle of Jutland), HMS *Monarch* (a 22,000-ton Orion-class battleship built and launched by Armstrong Whitworth in 1911), HMS *Hercules* (a 20,000-ton Colussus-class dreadnought built by Palmers and launched in 1910) and HMS *Queen Mary* (a 26,000-ton battlecruiser built by Palmers and launched in 1913. The *Queen Mary* blew up and sank at Jutland with the loss of 1,266 of her crew, there were only eighteen survivors).

Local newspaper coverage sought to keep the Newcastle public informed with extensive maps showing the route of the German invasion through Belgium and France and also naval maps which illustrated the possible risk

The launch of HMS Hercules *at Jarrow in 1910, a site frequently repeated along the Tyne during the war.* (Newcastle City Library)

to Great Britain if Germany was successful. Major battles were also widely reported but were obviously subject to heavy censorship and often gave quite incorrect and overly-positive reports which were quite often contradicted by the extensive and mounting casualty lists which were also published. The newspapers sometimes reported with considerable anti-German feeling and were not averse to publishing quite blatant propaganda pieces; thus the local coverage of the Battle of Mons contained the sub-headline 'German Barbarities' and went on to describe how German troops were mistreating both British soldiers and foreign civilian populations.

In contrast to Yorkshire and Lancashire, a journalist on *The Times* reporting on Britain in wartime found that the war was much more evident on Tyneside. Because of the vital war industries on Tyneside and the perceived vulnerability of the area to naval bombardment or even an enemy landing, the military presence in the area was much more evident and civilian attitudes were more circumspect. However, the reporter was at pains to make clear that civilian life continued as normal but that things were 'not quite normal'.[23]

Many threats to wartime production on Tyneside were considered and the government took these threats very seriously indeed. One of the greatest perceived threats was that of drunkenness affecting the workforce and therefore impacting on productivity. The Temperance Movement had not experienced great success on Tyneside and the public houses benefitted from brisk trade. The main threat to many of these in Newcastle was the growth of the popularity of working men's clubs; with over fifty trading in the city.

Worries over excessive drunkenness continued to be a recurring theme in the first months of the war and cases regularly appeared in the local press. In one case, just days after the outbreak of war Mr Thomas Hindhaugh, the publican of the Dudley Arms in Dudley, was charged with permitting drunkenness on his premises and with continuing to serve intoxicating liquor to a drunken man. The prosecution case was, however, completely undermined by the testimony of a miner who had been a witness to the supposed offence. The witness claimed that the supposedly drunken man, was sitting with his elbow on a table and his pipe held in his other hand in a 'pitmatic' manner but could easily have, 'drunk ten more'. As a result of this conflicting evidence all charges were dropped and both of the accused were acquitted.[24]

Less than a month later a 38 year-old labourer, John Lewis, fell afoul of the new strictness surrounding drunkenness and the wartime situation. Mr Lewis was reportedly drunk and had 'interfered with' (presumably verbally abusing

HMS Queen Mary. *Built at Jarrow in 1913 and sunk at the Battle of Jutland in 1916.* (Newcastle City Library)

or accosting) the sentry guarding a waterworks. Taking a harsh line the assizes sentenced Mr Lewis to twenty-one days of hard labour without the option of a fine.[25]

In fact, the local authorities had already prepared for this and had reacted speedily to the declaration of war by ordering every licensed house in Newcastle to close at 9.00pm. Thus one of the most marked differences in Newcastle from other cities was that by 9.30pm the city was almost deserted and by 10.00pm even the working-class districts were in darkness with the majority of people in bed. This change had been accepted willingly and with 'unquestioning loyalty'.[26]

Many would question this reporters view, however, as it seems clear that there was in fact considerable opposition to the times. The attitude of the authorities towards the working class perceived over-indulgence in alcoholic drink persisted throughout the war and could at times assume ridiculous proportions and demonstrate a very condescending attitude. The proposal by the council to limit the hours of public houses and to order their closure between the hours of 9.00pm and 8.00pm were met with derision and anger in many quarters. The Newcastle & Gateshead Licensed Victuallers Association expressed the anger and concern of its membership when they passed a strong resolution against the proposed measures and stated that to close public houses during these hours would deprive many hard working men of necessary refreshment upon the end of a hard shift.

The people of Newcastle, it was reported, demonstrated marked enthusiasm, excitement and loyalty at the outbreak of war. The miners in particular were singled out for praise by *The Times*. It reported that although an estimated 40,000 Northumberland miners were left idle in the previous week they had, through their union, declared themselves solidly behind the government and there has been no complaint from the miners. Indeed the miners had reacted angrily to a memorandum sent from an official of the Northumberland Miners' Association which declared that Britain should remain neutral. The miners were aware that in the first weeks and months of the war there would be too many miners and so they immediately set their hands to other important work. The Northumberland Miners' Association immediately placed its idle members at the disposal of farmers who were short of labourers at harvest. Indeed, the association went further and organized a scheme with Armstrong College to teach miners agricultural practices.

The patriotic fervour and the wish to aid the dependants of those who were serving extended beyond the council and individual companies to individuals. It would have been very welcome when Newcastle doctors agreed that they would provide free medical attendance to dependents of those on active service and that chemists would provide dispensing at cost price.

Of prime concern to the people of Newcastle was the possibility of increasing food prices which would result in a change to their standards of living or shortages. Some popular brands were at pains to keep their prices at pre-war levels and to reassure their customers. For example, Oxo (which had a branch office in Newcastle) took out a large advertisement in *The Times* which declared no rise in prices and that even though there was increased demand it had put in place measures sufficient to guarantee supplies. The advert also had a patriotic side as the illustration showed the product being loaded onto London omnibuses for transport to a Red Cross hospital.

The lack of available foodstuffs ensured that tensions remained high among many of the Newcastle working class and in the second week of August this

OXO advert, Sunderland Daily Echo, 19 August 1914.

Ever popular with the troops, tobacco was heavily advertised throughout the war: North Eastern Daily Gazette, 7 August 1914.

tension boiled over into an aggressive confrontation. The incident started with claims that Mr Miller, a grocer on Adelaide Terrace had ordered flour but was overcharging. A gang of youths overturned a cart which was outside Mr Miller's shop and a large and angry crowd of several thousand gathered. At first the crowd merely sang patriotic songs such as 'Rule Britannia' and the national anthem before more unruly elements once again took charge and the windows of Miller's shop were broken by stones; a second shop was also attacked with stones accompanied by more patriotic singing. The incident then took on a more sinister turn when the crowd turned its fury on a pork butchers' shop (possibly German owned) and the premises of a pawnbroker. The police on duty could do little as they were severely outnumbered and, despite reinforcements arriving, the crowds did not disperse until the early hours of the morning. This sparked further scenes of unrest over the next few days as a number of pork butchers' shops were attacked (this trade was dominated by Germans and Austrians, many were naturalized British citizens).

The rising cost of food also had a devastating outcome for many of the pets belonging to those who could no longer afford to feed them. Forced to prioritize, many simply gave their pets away or abandoned them. By early September, the Dog & Cat Shelter at Haymarket Lane was reporting that it had been inundated with animals that could no longer be cared for. The shelter had received ninety-eight dogs and sixty cats and had been forced to destroy sixty-two dogs and forty cats.

These increases in the cost of living at the start of the war had varying effects on Newcastle families. For those who had members working in munitions industries (especially armaments manufacturing) the influx of orders combined with higher wages meant that they could keep pace. For those who had family members who were out of work, in the army or employed in industries in which the war had caused an initial slump, the increases meant further hardships as they struggled to buy food for the larder essential to keep adults and children in good health. It is no wonder that some residents reacted with anger, which occasionally erupted into violence, when they believed that shopkeepers and others were making large profits at their expense. Grocers in particular appear to have been targets for resentment as it was widely believed that there were a significant number who were engaged in profiteering and in encouraging shortages in order to push prices up even further.

Newcastle's council clearly recognized the dangers that could arise if there was an emergency such as supplies being completely cut off or an invasion force landing. The Lord Mayor petitioned for the assembly of a large body of workers who would assume responsibility for the distribution of emergency supplies in such a case. The city police also received notice that they were to advertise for and, if necessary, call up special constables. The mayor also immediately set up a war-relief fund and such was the patriotic fervour among 'the great and the good' of the city, that by the end of August the total raised stood at £21,784 11s 5d. Ordinary charitable work also continued and on 6 August the West End Poor & Aged People's Summer Holiday Club organized thirty large omnibuses to take approximately 1,000 elderly people to Lambton Park where they were welcomed by and made guests of Lord Durham and Lady Lambton.

Upon the announcement of war, it was clear that considerable disruption would result and although Newcastle was a relatively small and compact city with a largely British population it still contained a significant number of foreign nationals. The dislocation caused by the declaration of war resulted in a significant number of Newcastle residents of foreign birth looking to leave the country. In order to facilitate this exodus, the foreign consulates in Newcastle remained open throughout the weekend so that their nationals could make arrangements to leave the country. Those seeking to leave included enemy aliens, it was estimated that there were approximately 100 German citizens of military-service age living in Newcastle and a number left to join the German Army. There were also people from neutral countries and allies. In Newcastle, over twenty French nationals who were eligible for conscription into the French Army made their arrangements and left on Monday. They included well-known men such as Monsieur Moubouissin who had taught French at Rutherford College (Moubouissin was later killed while serving as a Lieutenant in the French Army) and shipping agent Mon. Raillard who left to join his regiment in which he had previously served.

The presence of enemy aliens had been an increasingly sensitive subject and there had been anti-German disturbances in the city prior to the war. Fears over the presence of German citizens, naturalized or not, could run rampant especially when a patriotic popular press encouraged people to be on the alert for possible spies. On the second day of the war, a suspected spy was remanded in custody after being arrested in Newcastle and accused of observing naval yards and to have been making maps and lists of Tyneside shipyards. The accused, Frederick Sukowski, was a 26 year-old man who was said to have been born in East Prussia.

Upon the announcement of war, the security around key installations and locations was immediately tightened and many a hapless sightseer was challenged and even arrested under suspicion of spying. A dramatic incident took place on the Tyne when a riverboat, partially loaded with wood, steamed too close to three motor-torpedo boats which were moored at Palmers. The crew of the riverboat ignored warnings to heave to and instead turned and steamed downstream despite the navy firing a warning shot across the bows of the vessel. Three naval officers quickly commandeered one of Palmers' steam launches (*Turtle*) along with her two civilian crewmen and set off in pursuit but collided with a hopper in mid-river and sank. The crew abandoned ship and four were rescued but, sadly, one the civilians, Peter Mulholland, was drowned while the riverboat escaped and was never traced.

By the end of the first week of the war, the army had arrested several German citizens in Newcastle but the eagerness of the authorities to crack down on possible spying and suspicious behaviour resulted in some mistaken arrests and unfortunate incidents. During the early afternoon of 8 August, a young man was arrested by two members of the territorial force who believed that he had been acting suspiciously and that, given he looked foreign, was suspected of being a German. After some investigations it was revealed that the man was in Britain legally and that he was in fact a Russian-Finn. Other mistakes could prove considerably more dangerous. This was the case when members of a territorial battalion of the Northumberland Fusiliers who were responsible for guarding the reservoir at Benwell accidentally fired a shot which shattered the window of the nearby Benwell Park Lodge and narrowly missed the resident, Mrs MacDonald and her chauffeur. On hearing of the incident, a reporter from the newspaper made enquiries but was followed by members of the army unit, then challenged and subsequently arrested by the commanding officer on suspicion of spying. The reporter was eventually allowed to plead his case and after showing his identity documentation he was, somewhat reluctantly, released.

Anti-German feeling combined with spy mania continued throughout August and resulted in at least two further cases. Mr Paul Weise, a shipbroker who resided at Nuns Moor Road in Fenham, was brought before the court after being arrested in the vicinity of St Joseph's catholic school in Benwell. The school was at the time being used to house prisoners of war and enemy aliens. Mr Weise was found to have in his possession a means of communicating with Germany for business purposes but it was alleged that this could also be used for spying and, as Mr Weise was an enemy alien, he was remanded before being deported. Just days later Mr Karl Stubenroll, a 27 year-old submarine engineer and draughtsman of Austrian birth, was charged with having obtained notes and documents relating to submarines which could be of use if transmitted to the enemy. Upon referral to the Home Office it was decided that the charges be dropped but that Mr Stubenroll be re-arrested and served with a deportation order.

The declaration of war had also left many British nationals stranded in mainland Europe with a large number of businessmen, for example, stranded. The initial disruption to shipping was problematic but as war insurance regulations were organized the Norwegian Legation was able to announce that the regular Norwegian Line run between Newcastle and Bergen would resume and be scheduled to run six times a week for passengers travelling to any destination in Norway or Sweden.

Newcastle had always had a large and keen sporting fraternity and in the early months of the war the attempt to maintain some semblance of normality remained. Football, although often maligned for being unpatriotic, remained popular and a large crowd watched Newcastle United being beaten by arch-rivals Sunderland at home in the final of the Sunderland Hospital Cup. During the first months of the 1914 season, Newcastle fans were watching a team which it seemed was superior to any team they had put out in the last three years with the clubs' three half-backs (Hewison, Wilfrid Low and Hay) being the star men along with Hudspeth (left-back), another star. The club also managed to raise substantial funds for the war effort by arranging collections before each match. The players training

Newcastle Utd away at Man City, 10 October 1914.

regime changed so that it included military drill and shooting practices on a makeshift rifle range set up at the Gallowgate end of the ground. The club paid for a Boer War veteran, Julius Askelund, to deliver shooting instruction and the players took part in rifle competitions as part of their training. Many of the players also joined the military and by 1915 some twenty-seven out of forty players on the clubs' books had signed up.[27] On 10 October, the team had drawn away against Manchester City and lay in sixth position in the league championship. The team was now treating its fans to a succession of exciting and goal-laden matches; beating Sheffield United four goals to three on 24 October.

By October, fears were rising, driven along by the local and national press, and also among the population of the city regarding the enemy alien population. It was believed that not enough was being done to control this group and that they represented a threat to security and to the war effort. As such the government was pressed to act, and on 23 October the press was able to report that police had been occupied throughout the night in rounding up ninety German and Austrian citizens who resided in various parts of Newcastle; a further twenty were arrested at Gateshead. The aliens were largely made up of hotel managers, commercial travellers and clerks.

Over the first wartime Christmas period this 'anti-alienism' was exacerbated after a German prisoner, John Jurgen Kuhr, was reported to have escaped from Newcastle Gaol on Sunday, 27 December. The authorities found evidence left in his cell that the prisoner had made a rope from his bedclothes and used this to drop from the prison wall. The police mounted a large-scale search and all shipping bound for continental ports was thoroughly searched before departure, while his description was widely circulated. After several days, Kuhr was found to still be inside the prison grounds; he had escaped from his cell by using a skeleton key but was then unable to escape from the main prison.

The Caring Professions

Immediately after war was declared, it became clear that the medical establishment would have to react with alacrity to receive the expected numbers of wounded servicemen who would be returning to Britain. Therefore, many civilian hospitals were largely or completely turned over to military use while large numbers of the wealthy individuals volunteered their own properties for use as hospitals or recuperation centres. However, this caused problems for the civilian sick as many found themselves released early from hospital or

A ward at Armstrong College. (Newcastle University)

facing cancelled operations. As this problem grew it came to the attention of many who had volunteered their premises; one, Lady Ridley of Blagdon Hall to the north of Newcastle, had volunteered to house twenty-five invalids from the Royal Infirmary along with necessary staff. The first group of patients arrived on or around 9 August but Lady Ridley urged others to follow her example. Once these patients had received treatment and, depending on the local situation, these beds would later be used for wounded soldiers who would be sent from the infirmary.

The military and civil authorities were desperately searching for sites which could be used as military hospitals. The first to be listed were the wards of civilian hospitals, but other buildings used in Newcastle included asylums, small specialist hospitals, large private buildings and stately homes. A quickly identified site was the buildings of Armstrong College which was home to a number of faculties from Durham University, including the medical school. The decision was quickly taken to convert the college into a military hospital and work was undertaken by local companies. By the first week of September, the conversion to a military hospital (the 1st Northern General Hospital) had been completed.

The first casualties were not long in arriving and soon large numbers of wounded were being transported from the Front to hospitals in Newcastle. The newspapers initially attempted to keep up with recording the influx of wounded; on 23 September *The Times* was reporting that 107 men had arrived at the 1st

Northern General Hospital (Armstrong College); many of them seriously injured.[28]
The hospital was supported by the local authorities and by charitable donations of
money, equipment, food and gifts for the wounded. The hospital was staffed by
regular members of the Royal Army Medical Corps (RAMC) and by volunteers
from a number of organizations including the First Aid Nursing Yeomanry Corps
(FANY).

It was often said that the civilians of Newcastle were as much a part of
the war as those serving on the frontlines and, indeed, the population was
encouraged to believe this by the authorities and by the press. This point was
forcibly driven home by the German naval bombardment of several north-
east coastal towns (most famously Scarborough and Whitby) which caused a
large number of casualties. The events not only reinforced the growing hatred
of the enemy but also helped to strengthen resolve and provided the press
and the government with a golden propaganda opportunity. The bombardment
of the east coast had a salutary effect on the citizens of Newcastle who had
been forcibly reminded of their own vulnerability, but if anything the event

*Dr Ethel Williams
was a well-known
GP in Newcastle
and a leader of the
local Suffragette
Movement. During
the war she
played an active
role on a number
of committees
providing aid
to men and
women involved
in war work:
Newcastle Journal,
7 September 1914.*

Wounded soldiers at Newcastle in their red and blue 'wounded' uniforms.
(Newcastle University)

appeared to stiffen morale and make the populace more determined; it also considerably boosted anti-German feeling within the city.

As the end of the year approached the people of Newcastle had, by and large, adapted well to the initial wartime conditions. Charity efforts to raise funds for a number of causes (mainly supporting the armed forces and their dependents, the Red Cross and other medical support charities and also some funds to support allied countries) were in full swing and being enthusiastically supported by the majority. The war had brought a miniature boom to the Newcastle economy and many workers who had initially believed that the war might see them being put out of work had in fact benefited from higher wages; although at the cost of longer hours, lack of union support and the loss of drinking time. Many of those who had been unemployed or who believed that their jobs were at risk had by this time signed up for service and were either awaiting the call or were already under training at locations all around the country. The first wartime Christmas was greeted with almost the usual level of celebration with church attendances up, but increasing food prices had an impact on Christmas lunch for many people. The thoughts of Newcastle residents were never far from the suffering of those involved in the fighting and the publicity attracted by the reporting that 850 wounded men would be housed in the 1st Northern General Hospital at Armstrong College over Christmas Day, many of them far from their own homes, ensured that an appeal for donations of gifts met with a generous response.

Notes

1   In 1911, the population stood at 250,825 (an increase of 161,669 from the 1851 total).

2   See Barke. Mike: T*he People of Newcastle: A Demographic History* in Colls.
R & Lancaster. B (eds): *Newcastle upon Tyne. A Modern History* (2001), pp 141-154.

3   Hewitson, T.L: *Weekend Warriors: From Tyne to Tweed* (2006). pp. 127.

4   Cooke. Captain C.H. MC: *Historical Records of the 16th (Service) Battalion Northumberland Fusiliers* (1923), pp. 1-2.

5   Ibid.

6   Sheen, John: *Tyneside Irish. 24th, 25th, 26th and 27th (Service) Battalions of Northumberland Fusiliers* (2010), Kindle Edition, Loc 260-274.

7   Ibid: Loc 279.

8   *Newcastle Daily Chronicle*, 5 August 1914, pp. 5.

9   *Newcastle Daily Chronicle*, 6 August 1914, pp. 5.

10   *Newcastle Daily Chronicle*, 5 August 1914, pp. 2.

11   *The Times*, 7 September 1914, pp. 3.

12   Vall, Natasha: *The Emergence of the Post-Industrial Economy in Newcastle 1914-2000*, in Colls, Robert and Lancaster, Bill (eds): *Newcastle upon Tyne. A Modern History* (2001), pp. 49.

13   *The Times*, 7 August 1914, pp. 2.

14   *The Times*, 30 September 1914, pp. 11.

15   *The Times*, 2 October 1914, pp. 4.

16   Ibid, 15 December 1914, pp. 5.

17   Ibid.

18   *Newcastle Weekly Chronicle*, 22 August 1914, pp. 8.

19   *The Times*, 17 August 1914, pp. 3.

20   Ibid, 16 September 1914, pp. 8.

21   Ibid, 4 August 1914, pp. 4.

22   *Newcastle Weekly Chronicle*, 9 September 1914, pp. 5.

23   *The Times*, 17 August 1914, pp. 3.

24   *Newcastle Daily Chronicle*, 6 August 1914, pp. 4.

25   *Newcastle Weekly Chronicle*, 5 September 1914, pp. 5.

26   *The Times*, 17 August 1914, pp. 3.

27   Joannou, Paul: *United: The First Hundred Years...and some. The Official History of Newcastle United FC 1882 to 1995* (1995), pp. 108-109.

28   *The Times*, 23 September 1914, pp. 4.

CHAPTER 2

1915
The Deepening Conflict

A People's War?

As the casualties mounted towards the end of 1914 people began to realize the full impact of the fighting in France and Belgium and, at the command of the King and Queen along with the churches, a national day of prayer was announced in the form of a special intercession service. For people seeking comfort and reassurance the idea proved to be very popular with the result that, in Newcastle, 50,000 copies of the form of service were ordered. During church services, collections were undertaken for the relief of the sick and wounded. The service at United Wesleyan church in east Newcastle raised the sum of £7 12 shillings and 6 pence while a service at the church of St Mary the Virgin in Rye Hill raised over £8.

Newcastle continued its widely known dedication to contributing considerable sums to war-time charitable concerns with the population making donations to appeals both large and small. Many small companies, clubs and organizations had collection boxes and carried out regular initiative to raise funds for various causes. A popular fund was for the sick and wounded was run by *The Times* newspaper which regularly published results of the sums raised. For example, in February 1915, the Byker and Heaton Conservative Working Men's Club raised over £7 for the running costs of motor ambulances. The Lady Mayoress' fund to build new motor ambulances was particularly successful and by early July it had raised the sum of £1,350 and the ambulances were being built locally.

The execution of Nurse Edith Cavell generated great sympathy and many wished to raise some form of lasting monument to her memory and sacrifice.

Amongst the many charitable days that were arranged in Newcastle several supported Britain's allies. This was the Mayor being presented with his flag by Miss Doris Bibby on Russian Flag Day: Daily Mirror, 7 June 1915.

Motor car built by Armstrong Whitworth's, vehicles similar to this were used as ambulances. (Newcastle City Library)

ILITARY HOSPITAL, HIGH TEAMS, GATESHEAD 2570

A military hospital, this one at nearby Gateshead but indicative of several which were created at Newcastle. (Newcastle City Library)

In Newcastle, a scheme was begun to build an institution or hospital ward to care for disabled sailors, soldiers and munitions workers. Several meetings were held and letters sent out; by the end of the war the fund had raised almost £800. In order to raise funds for the Nurse Cavell Memorial Fund for Disabled Nurses two poems, *Wor Contemptible British Army* and *The Big Push*, written by a local man (Charles Anderson of Burradon Colliery) were printed and sold around Newcastle.[29]

As Newcastle was a hub for both industry and military activity the city saw its fair share of visitors. Rudyard Kipling was a visitor to the city in 1915, while J.B. Priestley served at Tynemouth with 10th Battalion; Duke of Wellington's Regiment and was briefly billeted in Newcastle. Priestley formed a very low opinion of the city and its inhabitants; his foremost complaint being the harshness of the local dialects.[30]

The city also saw its fair share of unwilling visitors due to the activities of the enemy. As the number of vessels being sunk in the North Sea increased due to submarine warfare and the increasing amount of mines large numbers of seamen were sometimes landed at Newcastle after their vessel had been sunk. A typical example of this was when the 6,400-ton Norwegian steamer

SS *American* was torpedoed on the night of Saturday, 1 May. The crew of thirty-nine took to the boats and were later picked up by the Norwegian mail steamer SS *Sterling* which was en-route to Newcastle. The *Sterling* was pursued and halted by a German submarine and after discussions ascertained that there were no British citizens on board was allowed to proceed on her way. On 3 May, thirty-nine Norwegian sailors from the mail steamer were landed at Newcastle.

Military Hospitals

With the fighting producing more casualties than had previously been anticipated it became necessary to find more hospital bed space. Several hospitals and institutions in Newcastle were converted to this use and gave great wartime service. The Newcastle Lunatic Asylum at Coxlodge (now St Nicholas NHS Psychiatric Hospital) was one building which appeared ideal for use as a military hospital and the visiting committee approached the military to gauge their interest. The approach was met with a positive response and preparations were immediately begun to assess the feasibility of such a conversion. The patients in the asylum were sent to other asylums around the north of England but there were extended discussions after authorities in North Riding and Cumberland demanded payment for accepting the Newcastle patients. A way around this was found by making space available for an extra sixty patients (thirty of each sex) at Stannington, Morpeth and Sunderland.[31]

By the start of April, preparations were at an advanced stage with Northern Command having inspected the asylum and declared it, somewhat optimistically, as perfectly suited for conversion. Changes which would have to be made were, however, quite extensive and included the building of an operating theatre, sterilizing rooms, an X-ray room and also annexes for the dining and recreation areas. Gas cookers would also have to be supplied in sufficient numbers as would bed-pan sluices and the construction of more water mains. It was agreed that the War Office would be responsible for the majority of these alterations. By mid-April tenders had been put out for some equipment such as beds, lockers and bedding with local companies being approached to bid; further tenders were issued later in the month. It was also thought necessary to construct a new billet for the extra nursing staff. Staffing costs proved somewhat problematic as the War Office was only prepared to pay for staff from the RAMC while the committee was expected to fund the others.

A further blow fell when the medical superintendent of the asylum contacted the council to tender his resignation as he felt that he could not cope with the added burden of running a war-time hospital.[32] The council accepted this and approached the War Office to appoint a medical officer in charge of the hospital. The War Office moved quickly and a Colonel Prescott was appointed as officer in charge. The colonel immediately undertook a survey of the site and completed the list of required medical staff with advertisements being placed for an additional four civilian nurses and also clerks and dispensers, all to be appointed at competitive wages.[33] The colonel also agreed that the Free Church chaplain who had worked at the asylum should be kept on and a fee of £25 per week was agreed.[34]

Building work continued on the asylum, but when the committee made its monthly inspection in late April the contractor, Mr Alex Pringle, stated that good progress had been made in general but the isolation ward was behind schedule with almost no work having been carried out. Mr Pringle claimed that the main cause for this delay was the lack of available unskilled labour (although skilled labour was plentiful) and that he had advertised for extra men and had set those who were working on overtime. Progress had also been delayed by a small fire which had caused some limited damage. The committee was pleased with the progress that had been made and agreed to pay a bonus to Mr Pringle if he could complete the work by May instead of the original August deadline. Although Mr Pringle agreed to this, he later informed the committee that this had failed to take into account work on the electrical and hot-water systems.

Spurred on by the possibility of a bonus the contractor pushed the work on and by 19 May almost all of the building work, except the isolation ward, was complete. But in mid-June, a dispute between the Plumbers Association and the hot-water engineers working for Mr Pringle delayed some of the work. Mr Pringle also recommended that a new laundry should be installed and this was tendered out at a cost of approximately £500.

Colonel Prescott also made some command decisions at this time and petitioned for all of the male civilian attendants to be authorized to join the RAMC for home service only. He found that the majority of the men were quite willing to enlist on these terms. The male attendants successfully campaigned for the right to continue to receive bonuses for activities such as singing in the hospital choir or playing in the band. As a result of the favourable conditions almost all of the male attendants agreed to enlist. Colonel Prescott also decided that the initial proposal to build a railway line to transfer wounded directly to the hospital was not sustainable. Instead, a plan was put into place for the patients to be transferred by ambulance from the railway station at West Gosforth. In order to facilitate this, six motor ambulances were purchased and housed in a garage at Barras Bridge. This cost some £150 which was paid for by the council's volunteer transport fund. Colonel Prescott also oversaw the arrival of the many staff that would be required to man the hospital. Initially the orderlies were accommodated in tents in the grounds. The colonel was also at pains to point out to the council that where voluntary aid was forthcoming it should always be accepted.[35]

By mid-May, the committee was sufficiently confident with the progress of work that they decided to form a ladies' committee that would be tasked with providing comforts to patients and staff. These would include the provision of clothing and food, activities and visits to some of the ladies' homes by the less severely injured officers. Volunteers for the ladies' committee were sought from the wives and relations of the men on the main committee and an initial meeting was organized at the Mansion House.

Towards the end of May, the hospital was almost complete and further staff which included nurses and attendants also a chef and an assistant were employed and moved on site. Colonel Prescott also notified the committee that while the hospital had employed two masseurs a further four were required. By the end of July, the wages for staff amounted to £13,051 18 shillings and 7 pence. Extra bonuses were awarded to the staff to further encourage performance; employees earning less than 30 shillings per week being awarded 2 shillings and 6 pence; while those earning over 30 shillings but less than 40 shillings were awarded 1 shilling and 6 pence. Perhaps due to events in France, some of the RAMC personnel expressed a desire to be allowed to serve abroad if they wished and this was approved with their positions being kept open for their return. In order to provide cover, a further thirty probationary nurses were recruited.

By this point, the hospital was ready to receive patients and officially became the Northumberland No 1 War Hospital. After opening, the hospital was found to be so successful (and casualties so numerous) that a request was made to the council to agree to consider an extension to the hospital by building of extra ward blocks. After some debate, this was agreed to and eventually the approval was given for a further nine blocks which would increase capacity by 540 beds.[36]

A People's War?

Although there were suspicions of enemy aliens it seems that there was at this stage little aggression amongst the general populace. While the officer commanding the Tyne Defences had ordered that all enemy aliens be removed and excluded from a 4 mile radius of the coast this order did not apply to Newcastle. It was estimated that of over 500 enemy aliens who lived within the city limits at the commencement of the war, some 300 remained. A thorough

The Military Orthopaedic Centre at Leazes. Taken after the war the centre treated a large number of soldiers injured in the war. (Newcastle City Library)

system of supervision of any new arrivals or transients and the requirement to register at hotels and boarding houses combined with a card-registration scheme for all permanent non-British residents, enabled the police to keep an accurate track of aliens.

As the wartime situation became more serious, the people of Newcastle grew more suspicious of the enemy aliens in their communities. Fostered by a growing anti-spy mania which was given fuel by hysterical propaganda, newspaper campaigns and (usually false) accounts of German atrocities in France and Belgium, many began to consider the aliens, many of whom had been a part of the community for a long time, a serious threat. In May there were continuous, if low-level disturbances and protests. Most of these demonstrations were against German shopkeepers and tradesmen (probably more influenced by the need to get rid of competition than patriotic fervour) and in the second week of the month two butchers' shops in the east of the city were attacked and their windows broken. In Gateshead, there were similar incidents and prosecutions with a judge stating that if people continued to break the law in such a way it would end in murder.

Despite the worries over enemy aliens, at this stage of the war one of the greatest concerns to the people of Newcastle was the speed at which household necessities were increasing in price. This may also have been one of the main reasons behind the targeting of grocers and butchers' shops in disturbances. By mid-January, prices in the city were higher than they had been at any point in the war with a sack of corn having increased by 2 shillings and 6 pence per sack. In the previous weeks, there had been a dramatic rise in the price of all cereals with flour being priced at 2 shillings and 4 pence per stone (14lb) as compared to just 10 pence in January 1914. Meat, bacon, butter and tea had all increased in price by 3 pence per lb; cheese had increased by 2 pence and sugar by 1 penny with other necessary commodities increasing by between 1 and 2 pence. The working class of the city were becoming increasingly concerned over these rises as they depended on such necessities as the mainstay of their nourishment. The Newcastle Trades Council were also worried and at a meeting in mid-January, they condemned the increases and the greed of those responsible for them and contacted local their local MP to protest.

Such rises led to friction within the population as it was felt that the working classes were being hit hardest by the increases in the price of vital foodstuffs, while the wealthy and the middle classes could still afford to purchase and, in some cases, to hoard supplies. There was also increasing anger displayed against those who were felt to be making inappropriate profits from exploiting the wartime situation. Also there were increasing numbers of people urging the government to take control of the supply and pricing of vital necessities.

On Saturday, 13 February, a meeting involving trade unions, socialist groups and industrial workers organizations and addressed by members of the Labour Party was held in Newcastle (other meetings were held in other cities) to protest against the increasing living costs (especially the rising prices of fuel and food) and the effect that this was having on the civilian working class. There was considerable condemnation of the government and its failure to ensure that the civilian population was looked after in addition to members of the forces. Further appeals were made to the government to find some way of relieving the poor of the rising costs of living. This was the first sign that people were still willing to speak out when what was perceived as unfair costs were being passed on to them, despite the wartime situation. Newcastle was not known as a militant city with the Labour Party usually playing second fiddle to the Liberals in elections but the industrial workers were now in a position of some strength as they realized that wartime demand for their services meant that their work was worth considerably more and was of great importance.

In an effort to maintain moral standards and to ensure efficiency amongst workers a campaign was launched, following the King's example, to limit or eliminate completely the consumption of alcohol. Newcastle councillor and shipyard owner George Lunn was chair of the Newcastle Education Committee and led the calls for abstinence. Councillor Lunn pushed for the creation of a King's League which would consist of people who voluntarily agreed to abstain for the duration of the war. The league would also campaign for greater abstinence amongst the workforce in Newcastle and Tyneside. Councillor Lunn found early support from the vicar of Newcastle, Canon Gough, who praised the actions of the King and urged the people of Newcastle to follow the example. The church continued to be a firm backer of campaigns to limit consumption of alcohol and Newcastle Presbytery voted a resolution promising backing to any measure which the government took to limit drinking (clearly they were supportive of the total prohibition of sales of alcohol). Ironically the Lord Mayor of Newcastle, John Fitzgerald, was a brewer and bottler who had built up his business and acquired a large number of public houses and hotels since his arrival from Tipperary in 1878.

Given the industrial importance of Newcastle and Tyneside it is surprising that the Germans did not make more of a concerted effort to directly attack the region. The biggest threats came from seaborne raiding but by 1915 the most widely feared form of attack was from the air by means of the huge Zeppelins of the German Imperial Navy. Just after 8.00pm on 14 April trawlers identified the Zeppelin Z.9 approaching the north east coast from the direction of Heligoland. The Z.9, captained by *Kapitänleutnant* Mathy, was one of the newest available to the Germans and was 515ft in length and its three engines could reach speeds of over 40 mph. The Zeppelin was again spotted by Captain Jewels of the Blyth based tug 'Jupiter' and lights were extinguished in North Shields and Newcastle.[37] It was believed that the raid was aimed at the Armstrong works but the crew became disoriented in the dark skies (Blyth seems to have been a common location for Zeppelins to make landfall) mistaking the estuary of the Wansbeck for the Tyne and instead bombs were dropped seemingly at random around the area with incendiaries exploding at Choppington, Wallsend, Seatonburn, Annitsford, Killingworth and Bedlington. No one was injured and damage was said to be very light. Four bombs were dropped on the industrially important suburb of Wallsend and one started a house fire which was extinguished quite easily while two others fell on railway lines but did no appreciable damage while the final bomb landed in the river. There was some disruption to routine, however, as all electricity was cut as a precaution, trams were halted, the Great Northern (Kings Cross to Aberdeen) train was held at Central Station and rail traffic of all sorts briefly disrupted. The occupants of the house in Wallsend were

The busy junction of Westgate Road and Clayton Street in 1915. On the right can be seen The Picture House which eventually became The Gaumont. (Newcastle City Library)

uninjured but had a lucky escape as the incendiary exploded in a room which was used as a bedroom for the family's young boy. It was said in the press that the people of the area remained calm throughout the raid and that, at Wallsend, there was absolutely no panic.[38]

A far more serious raid took place on the night of 15/16 June when a raid by a Zeppelin L10, captained by *Kapitänleutnant* Hirsch, dropped bombs aimed at Newcastle industries with bombs being dropped on a marine engineering works at Wallsend, Jarrow and Willington Quay. Between twelve and seventeen people were killed with twelve men working at the Palmers Yard at Jarrow being later commemorated on a plaque. Clearly Tyneside had become a target and following this raid it was belatedly decided that Newcastle needed stronger defences.

Despite the increasing hardships and the worries of many who had men serving abroad it seems that the majority of Newcastle residents, especially the upper and middle classes, remained buoyant in spirit and cheerfully resolute. Although Newcastle was in the area for which the Defence of the Realms Act called for a blackout this was laxly applied in the city itself when compared to coastal towns.

The Times journalist who stayed at the Station Hotel in January reported that the city was welcoming and bustling and with lights burning along the Quayside and in every city street and suburb. The reporter declared that the longer one stayed in the city the more encouraged one became such was the cheerfulness of the inhabitants despite the risk of bombardment and possible invasion. The hotel itself was popular in the evenings and saw a mix of those in military service, ladies wearing evening dresses and 'captains of industry and commerce' all mingled and presented an inspiring view of the city during wartime.[39]

Newcastle was traditionally a very keen sporting city with a proud tradition of local sporting heroes (especially from the Victorian era) and, for many of the residents, taking part or supporting sports was their primary form of relaxation. Sports such as bowling, athletics, cycling, horse racing and football were universally popular while golf, cricket and rugby union found popularity amongst the wealthier classes. Many of these sports suffered during the war due to facilities being taken over for military use

Newcastle born Bombardier Dance (51st Brigade, Royal Field Artillery) after winning the Military Cross-Country Race at Aldershot against 800 competitors: Daily Record, 1 February 1915.

or by members of local clubs joining up or simply not having the amount of free time that they had in pre-war years.

Throughout 1915 the North-East Coast Armaments Committee was seeking ways to bring about a decline in absenteeism at the important munitions works in Newcastle and saw the continuation of horse racing meetings in the area to be potentially detrimental to munitions output. The committee thus held a meeting to discuss the possibility of abandoning and banning race meetings in the north-east. At the beginning of May, the committee communicated its intentions to the Jockey Club who immediately contacted the committee asking which meetings it wished to be abandoned. The committee expressed the opinion that all the fixtures at Newcastle (and Redcar and Stockton) were abandoned for the duration of the war and that other nearby meetings be assessed as to the effect they could have on armament work. The Jockey Club was quickly supportive and it was announced on 10 May that the summer meeting at Newcastle had been abandoned.

The sport that helped define Newcastle was, of course, football. The popularity of Newcastle United had caught the imagination of the city from 1900 and huge crowds could usually be guaranteed; aided by the fact that the club had gone through its golden period in the pre-war Edwardian era. In the years 1904 to 1909, the club won the league three times and appeared in five FA Cup finals. For many of the working class of Newcastle supporting the magpies was a key part of their life. Throughout the early months of 1915 football continued to be a source of entertainment and relaxation for many in Newcastle. Despite growing calls for the season to be abandoned and for all footballers to join up (even though a large number already had) Newcastle United continued to attract large crowds to St James' Park with many of the spectators being members of Kitchener's army dressed in khaki while the club allowed wounded servicemen from the converted hospital at Rutherford College to view the matches from the directors' enclosure and centre pavilion seating areas; many of these young Tynesiders had been wounded in the fighting at Mons. The men witnessed some exciting matches, thanks largely to an extended FA Cup run which ended with finalists Chelsea beating the 'Magpies' in front of a crowd of almost 50,000 at St James.

The Lord Mayor used the football matches to hold rallies at St James' Park in order to raise funds for the war effort and for causes such as Indian soldiers, the Belgian Relief Fund and the Serbian Relief Fund and Red Cross. The assembly of large crowds of men, inspired by those around them already in uniform and the patriotic fervour of being part of a large crowd proved to be a useful recruitment ground too. At the end of the season all football was suspended and players were released from their contracts. Many from Newcastle United immediately volunteered for service with the army while others became involved with vital wartime industry. Thus Frank Hudspeth and 'Jock' Finlay found work in the munitions industry while several others went down the pits. Many of those who had joined up saw active service during the war with former players Curtis Booth and Alex Higgins serving in France with the Durham Light Infantry, Bill Bradley in the Tank Corps and others in the Royal Engineers, Army Service Corps, Royal Navy and, inevitably, the Northumberland Fusiliers.[40]

One measure which could be relied upon to give a short-term boost to morale and encourage the people of Newcastle that their sacrifices were appreciated was the visit of a dignitary. On 19 May the King (accompanied by Lord Stamfordham, Major Clive Wigram and Vice-Admiral Sir Colin Keppel) visited Newcastle for a two day tour. On the first day His Majesty's itinerary included an extensive tour of the shipyards and engineering works of Tyneside. Emerging from Central Station just before ten in the morning the King was greeted by a large cheering crowd who were eager to show their loyalty. The King was presented to the Lord Mayor and other members of the council before undertaking his tour by train and steamer. At every destination the King took care to show an interest in the ongoing work and to talk to selected workers and he was met with warm applause and cheering at every destination. On the next day the King, accompanied by Lord Kitchener, Sir Colin Keppel and others, toured the munitions works of Armstrong Whitworth at Scotswood and Elswick before they inspected a large body of soldiers on the Town Moor during the afternoon. During his tour of Armstrong-Whitworth, the King took time to speak to and praise a number of workmen and to encourage them in their efforts. He afterwards addressed members of the North-East Coast Armaments Committee and asked them to convey his appreciation to the workmen and to urge them to even further efforts in the national cause. Lord Kitchener reinforced this view, expressed his own appreciation and urged the necessity of even greater output of munitions. Despite the fact that there had been little or no publicity an extremely large, but orderly, crowd thronged the rout the King would take to the Town Moor with the Police and members of the Civilian Training Corps being used to keep the crowds back. The mounted King was escorted onto the Moor by a guard of honour drawn from the Officers Training Corps and saluted onto the field with a fanfare. After an inspection the King, Lord Kitchener and others took the podium and accepted the salute and march-past of the troops. Lord Kitchener departed from Central Station shortly before 5.00pm and was seen off by cheering crowds. Overall the people of Newcastle and Tyneside seem to have been very supportive of their monarch at this point in the war and the visit certainly served its aims of boosting morale in the city.

Due to the greater restriction placed upon civilian activities it became increasingly easy for an otherwise law-abiding civilian populace to be criminalized as they fell afoul of rules, regulations and laws which they more often than not were not even aware of. In Newcastle there was great sensitivity around the armaments and shipbuilding industries and around the military activities within the city and on the river. Two cinema operators fell afoul of defence regulations when in February they decided to shoot film of military vessels on the Tyne. The two were arrested and prosecuted with the film being confiscated. The men, Stanley Dorman of Gosforth and Edwin Joseph Johnson of Newcastle, claimed at their trial a month later that the pictures were not to be used outside of Britain and that they had sought permission of the Board of Film Censors. Despite this both men were found guilty and fined the sums of £10 12 shillings and £25 respectively.

Fraudulent claiming also became a serious issue with some enlisted men claiming sums to which they were not entitled and one Newcastle man, Albert Joseph Brown, was summonsed in London after being accused, with his mother, of attempting to defraud the Admiralty. Mr Brown had enlisted in the Naval Division and claimed on is separation allowance form that before joining he had been allowing his mother who was a widow in Newcastle the sum of 12 shillings and 6 pence per week from his wage working as a traveller for a Newcastle based firm. His mother was asked to fill in a similar form and said that her son had been allowing her the sum of £1 per week. Upon investigation it was discovered that the firm did not exist and that Mr Brown had not been in regular employment for three years. The magistrate took a very dim view but as he did not believe there was any conspiracy between the two he did not send them to jail but instead fined each the sum of £5.

Other crimes were not related to the war but simply due to the character of the people involved with the stresses of wartime living no doubt exacerbating the situation. A serious example occurred on Christmas morning when a group of young men, who had no doubt been drinking, went around the rural village of Wylam singing Christmas Carols. Upon arriving at the farm of Mr John Nixon at around 1.00am they were met by Mr Dixon coming out of doors to confront them in a state of annoyance. One of the men wished him the compliments of the season and Mr Nixon said, 'I will 'merry Christmas' you" and thereupon shot one James Clark, who was wounded. Mr Nixon was subsequently arrested

So vast was the Elswick Works that it required its own firemen. This photograph is c.1910 and it is reported that a large number of these men joined up and subsequently lost their lives. (Newcastle City Library)

and charged before being brought before the court at Newcastle where he was remanded on bail.

Although spy mania was rife throughout the war not every suspicion was false. There were a number of traitors and pro-German's who were willing to betray their country out of loyalty to Germany or for money. Potentially, one such was a Newcastle woman named Margaret Henderson Smith who worked at the vital Elswick works of Armstrong-Whitworth's until being dismissed for suspicious behaviour in December. On 13 May she was formally charged under the Official Secrets Act with possessing a plan of a new fuse, transmitting information likely to be prejudicial to the safety of the Realm and with having attempted to gather information likely to be of use to the enemy. The prosecution alleged that Smith had sent a telegram from Sunderland on 18 April which read 'Impossible to get information necessary, wait till seven tonight, lights out last night, no clerks'. Upon questioning Smith admitted that she was a pro-German, that she was sworn to secrecy, that she was working for a man known to her as Carl Schmidt, who had accurate knowledge of all billeting contracts in the city, and that she had delivered the plan of the fuse, stolen from Elswick, to Schmidt. Smith admitted that she had then, on Schmidt's orders, travelled to Sunderland to discover when a captain with knowledge of new guns was departing for the front and that she had made enquiries of a private in the DLI as well as a colonel and major in the same regiment.[41] When Smith was again brought before the court a week later the Chief Constable of Newcastle stated that the Director of Public Prosecutions had instructed him that no charges would be forthcoming and the young woman was discharged; intriguingly, especially since the accused had made a confession, no other reason was given.

The works at Elswick were particularly security conscious due to the classified nature of much of the work undertaken there. In August, another worker was found to be in possession of classified and sensitive documents. Again, there were sinister hints at espionage as the offender this time was a German national. Mr William Sagar was charged at Newcastle Police Court with having entered a prohibited area. Sagar, a former master seaman had been employed at Elswick since April but had been born in Wustrow, Germany, but had endeavoured to erase this fact from his Board of Trade certificate. When his house was searched police found a copy of a document describing the dangers of enemy submarines. The document was marked private and confidential along with instructions that it was on no account to fall into enemy hands. He was sentenced to six months of hard labour.[42]

Recruitment

The willingness of eligible Newcastle men to join up still continued strongly into the second year of the war and recruitment continued to be brisk with several battalions of the Northumberland Fusiliers completed during the year and large numbers joining other regiments (the Durham Light Infantry and several Scottish regiments were all popular choices in the city). The people of the city continued to be proudly vocal about the city's recruitment record. Indeed government figures were used to encourage recruitment in those cities where it was thought eligible men were shirking. Throughout March the authorities in Leicester were particularly dismayed and used the example of Newcastle to try to boost recruitment; figures showed that 18.5 per cent of eligible Newcastle men had volunteered only 2.6 per cent in Leicester had.[43]

The Newcastle & Gateshead Commercial Exchange had raised three battalions at this point with another recruiting. The men of these battalions were mainly clerks and the Exchange was determined to ensure that these men and their dependants were as well looked after as possible; it was estimated 50 per cent of the men were married. To this end the Exchange had raised the sum of £25,000 to cover equipment, billeting and separation allowances with payments of approximately £300 per week available for wives and dependants. The total amount which was covered by the Exchange demonstrates the commitment of this organization and the Newcastle residents to the war effort with each battalion costing the organisation £4,000 after War Office payments.

In contrast the men of the Tyneside Scottish and Irish brigades had a much higher percentage of married men; estimated at between 75-80 per cent. A significant percentage of these units consisted of the rich recruiting grounds of former miners and labourers. The main recruitment office in Newcastle at Westgate Road was still busy and had over 12,000 men enrolled at the turn of the year (not including those who had signed up for the Commercials) with 8,784 being enrolled for service in Tyneside battalions and 3,469 for service with

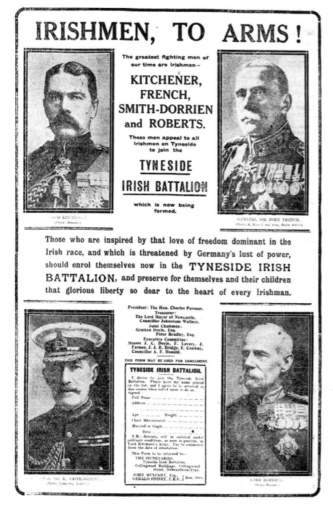

Recruiting posters for the local Pals' Battalions were a common feature in local newspapers: Sunderland Daily Echo, 24 October 1914.

The majority of churches played a substantial role in encouraging people to feel the war was justified. Sunday School groups played a key role in recruitment for many. (Newcastle City Library)

other regiments. The reasons for Newcastle men joining at this time were still exceptionally varied and ranged from economic concerns to a magnified sense of patriotism which was especially noticeable in the wake of the bombardment of Scarborough when there was a marked increase in the number of Newcastle men volunteering for the Naval Brigade. Some men left their families and travelled around the world in order to join the colours. One Scottish ship captain enlisted in the Tyneside Scottish at Newcastle having left his wife and children in the South Sea Islands, where he was the owner of a merchant schooner, and travelled home via Japan and Russia in order to enlist.

Young men continued to be exposed to anti-German propaganda as a means of encouraging their enlistment such as the meeting at the Newcastle Division of the Durham University Student Union held at Newcastle on 6 February which was addressed by Lord Gray. The sole content of Lord Gray's speech was the anti-British feelings of the German population. Lord Gray used the example of a German he had spoken with shortly before the war who had stated that every German's aim was to take Britain's empire from her and to insult the British national character by accusing them of being soft, lazy, unintelligent and disorganized. Such blatant use of propaganda on the young and impressionable proved to be a useful recruitment tool in Newcastle.

Then enthusiasm for enlisting was not however shared by all the residents of Newcastle and the fact that so many local men were signing up caused some resentment against those who had so far not volunteered. There was particular resentment aimed at rural workers who were under-represented and a belief that the reluctance of these men to volunteer resulted in a section of young and unmarried men who, while willing to serve under a fair system of conscription, were unwilling to sign up in the knowledge that others were likely to remain behind even though eligible.

Likewise, governmental errors and inefficiencies had led some within the council to complain. In early 1915, the government contacted the council to ask if any more men could be released from working for the corporation for service abroad. Although the corporation had already willingly released 500 men who were now serving they replied that there were a further 501 men who had said they were willing to serve voluntarily. The government had not responded since receiving this message and the Lord Mayor declared that he had heard of a similar case in another area where such men had been told to register with the labour exchange as if they were out of work. The Lord Mayor then went on to declare that no municipality had done more for the war effort than Newcastle and that, furthermore, the government was employing a large number of young men who were eligible for war service on the railways and others undertaking land valuation work for the government.

Industry and labour

The Commercial Exchange was increasingly concerned over the impact that the scarcity and cost of shipping space and the increase of railway-freight traffic were having on the local coal export business. At the start of the war coal exports dropped dramatically but had since picked up. However, the initial drop and the closure of traditional markets for the coal exported from the Tyne led to many miners joining the army as they believed that they would otherwise be left out of work. While exports had grown again since the initial downturn the prices were exorbitant and were leading to difficulties for local exporters. The price of shipping coal to Genoa had increased from 7 shillings per ton to 25 shillings and for Rouen from 4 shillings and 9 pence to 17 shillings. In contrast, the owners of merchant shipping were pleased with the situation as it meant they were making higher profits from cargoes to counterbalance the increased risks and insurance that they were facing. Many in the coal trade wanted the government to make available interned German shipping for freight trade but this proposal was not welcomed universally by Newcastle shipping companies and the issue led to heated debates amongst the members of the Commercial Exchange. The situation was resolved when the Admiralty declared its intention to make the steamers available for the coal trade by putting the thirty-three steamers, including the *Henry Furst* which had been detained at Newcastle in 1914, into the open market under the management of Newcastle-based shipping companies and making them available to the highest bidder. The Admiralty felt that this was necessary to bring the costs of shipping coal down to a reasonable level for east coast companies, including several based in Newcastle or owned by Newcastle residents.

After several months of war had restricted trade and exports it was realized that the country was deficient in some areas of industry that was important to the war effort. Many dyes, for example, had been imported from Germany and while Switzerland was a possible alternative it was realized that British companies had fell behind. In order to kick-start this important industry the government offered financial incentives and, in Newcastle, the Commercial Exchange was quick to take the initiative and moved to establish works in the city for the production of aniline dyes.

The trade organizations of Newcastle maintained a healthy interest in then interests of their members throughout the war and in 1915 one of their longest campaigns finally bore fruit. Since 1901, the North-East Coast Institution of Engineers & Shipbuilders had campaigned for the engineering officers of the Royal Navy to be given full military rank and Lord Fisher had finally agreed. On 6 February, *The Times* published a letter signed by several members of the institution thanking and praising Lord Fisher and making him an honorary member. The signatories reveal how key a role this organization played in Newcastle and in the war effort; the signatories included Lord Armstrong, Sir Andrew Noble and Colonel R. Saxon White of Armstrong Whitworth, William Boyd of Wallsend Slipway & Engineering Co, Sir Benjamin Browne of R & W. Hawthorn, Leslie & Co, John Hunter of Swan, Hunter & Wigham Richardson, Summers Hunter of the North-Eastern Marine Engineering Co, and Sir Charles Parsons of Parson Marine Steam Turbine Co.

One reflection of the anger being felt by many over the rising living costs was a greater willingness of working men in Newcastle to attempt to secure higher wages and better working conditions. By mid-February the shipbuilding unions were agitating for a substantial increase in wages to cover the increased cost of living. A meeting with the north-east coast engineering employers resulted in the workers being offered 2 shillings per week immediately, followed by a further 1 shilling in six months if the war continued. The unions however had their own ideas and offered a counter-proposal to the employers. Unskilled labourers in the industry were also willing to make demands. At the time of the above meeting the unskilled labourers were petitioning for an unprecedented increase of 5 shillings per week on time rates and 15 per cent on piece work.

The higher wages being sought and paid in the shipyards was a growing cause for concern as employers and the press made allegations that the men were not working as hard as they could and that productivity was therefore suffering. It was alleged that men would work double shifts on Sundays when they were paid time and a half only to then take Monday off as they had already gotten 'two days pay for one days' work'. One Newcastle shipbuilder claimed that men employed on Admiralty work were only working forty hours per week as opposed to an average of fifty-three hours solely because of the higher rates of pay. Little in the way of concrete evidence was put forward for this however with *The Times*, local newspapers and employers bodies stating that the fact that there had been fewer merchant vessels launched in the first three months of the year as opposed to 1914 was explainable by the fact that all the available workers were being placed on government work building naval ships.

The Newcastle shipbuilders were increasingly concerned about their productivity falling due to lost time and gave a variety of reasons including the above high wages but also the effect that alcohol was having on their workforce. At the end of March, a deputation from the Shipbuilding Employers' Federation, with Tyneside firms prominent, suggested to the Chancellor that prohibition should be introduced for the duration of the war. The employers put forward figures suggesting that lost time was seriously affecting them, especially in the case of platers, riveters and drillers. The employers demonstrated that Monday was the worst day with a quarter of men being absent for the whole day. Although the employers admitted that drinking was not solely responsible and that drunkenness was not rife amongst their workers, there was a growing move to close the yards on Sundays.

The workers themselves blamed other causes, primarily the poor organization of riveting squads which caused groups of men to be idle because of one absence. They also argued that because of the arduous nature of much of the work it was physically impossible for men to continue at their jobs constantly while also working overtime and said that, because of the shortage of skilled workers, men who were unsuitable were being employed on Tyneside and that this was hindering performance.

Munitions workers from Armstrong-Whitworth's on a rare day out. (Newcastle City Library)

Amongst the munitions workers the accusations of drunkenness, which was levelled particularly at workers on the Tyne and Clyde, and slackness were received very badly and were seen as a slur on both the men themselves and on Newcastle. It seems that while the companies manufacturing shells and armaments had no complaints about their employees but the shipbuilders still complained about the problem of slacking and the unwillingness of some workers, particularly riveters, to increase their hours or to recognize the necessity of sacrifice in this time of national emergency. Employers did not agree that exhaustion was a factor in poor productivity but believed that, while actual drunkenness was low, the heavy ale drunk by the men led to a decrease in efficiency. The media campaign continued, however, and became increasingly patronising in tone. Shortly after a visit by the King and Lord Kitchener in which both had praised the Tyneside workforce for their efforts *The Times* published a piece headlined 'The Problem of Munitions' and in a sub-heading 'Lost Time, Overwork, and Drink' again alleged that the problem primarily affected the Tyne and the Clyde and stated, without giving evidence, that 'Tyneside is normally the most drunken district in England'. The paper went on to allege that the high wages and drunken behaviour therefore meant that in Newcastle, 'the war is taken light heartedly by people who were never so well off in their lives,' and attempts to reinforce this view by commenting on the large number of theatre and music hall advertisements in a local newspaper.[44] Such complaints from London based journalists who had little knowledge of Tyneside or other northern industrial centres were undoubtedly the cause of much resentment amongst the working classes as they would seem to accurately reflect the views of some of the middle and upper classes who read newspapers such as *The Times*.

Strike action also started to reappear despite the generally patriotic feeling present in the city. In March employees of the North-Eastern Railway Company came out on strike after demanding an increase of 1 shilling per day, which amounted to a 20 per cent wage increase, for the loading and conveying of goods. At this time the country was also witnessing ongoing strikes and disputes in Scotland, Liverpool and Northampton.

In April, a meeting was called at the request of Lord Kitchener to discuss the acceleration of the manufacture of munitions on the north-east coast. It was proposed that a committee be formed to further mobilize workers in this industry and in response to a War Office appeal for more men the Birmingham Corporation released over a thousand men to work in munitions in the North-East. The most obvious location for the meeting was at Newcastle as the city was the hub of munitions production in the North-East. The meeting was well attended by shipbuilders and trade union representatives and by Captain Power, RN, Captain Creed (representing Lord Kitchener), the Duke of Northumberland and Lord Durham. Lord Kitchener sent a memo to the Lord Mayor that increasing production of munitions was of the utmost urgency and that such an acceleration must be maintained throughout the war. The War Office came in for some criticism as it was felt a concerted appeal to the area should have been made at the outbreak of the war and that a mixed message had been sent when Lord Kitchener announced in February that he would have all the necessary munitions. Lord Durham also asked if this appeal was limited to Newcastle or applied to the wider North-East region and was told that Lord Kitchener, 'knew the shops were on Tyneside, that machinery and raw material were there, that the question of housing was not insoluble, and that there was a sufficient supply of skilled and unskilled labour which could be mobilized.'[45] The trade union representative and the Lord Mayor were more enthusiastic and declared that they would do their best to deliver Lord Kitchener's request. The Lord Mayor's proposal to form a North-East Coast Armaments Committee was unanimously approved.

Once approved the setting up of the committee was undertaken with all possible speed and later that week the members were selected (seven from the employers and seven representatives of the employees) and the first meeting set for the afternoon of Thursday, 15 April. Such was the enthusiasm of both employers and employees that a telegram was sent to Mr Asquith apprising him of the situation and assuring the government of 'their desire to assist in every way in accelerating the supply of munitions of war'. Although the committee had jurisdiction over the whole north-east coast it was clear that the vast majority of munitions were produced on the Tyne so it was decided that a significant part of their work would be in identifying how much labour could be moved from other districts to Newcastle. The

The Prime Minister addresses the Palace Theatre in Newcastle: Daily Mirror, 22 April 1915.

committee quickly came to the conclusion that production at Elswick could be substantially increased as the machinery was in place but there was a shortage of skilled labour. The commitment and patriotic enthusiasm of the workers was particularly welcomed in government circles with the local War Office representative, Captain Creed declaring, 'he was delighted with the action of the men in the matter, as they had promised to do everything that Lord Kitchener had asked'.[46] Clearly there was still a patriotic commitment to the war effort amongst the workers of Newcastle, particularly when the matter was of obvious relation to the successful prosecution of the war.

The creation of the committee gave a significant boost to the morale and patriotism of the people of Newcastle. This was particularly noted amongst those workers engaged in the armaments industries. It was quickly announced that Mr Asquith was to visit Newcastle in order to give a speech to the industrial workers who were engaged in vital munitions work. The meeting was to take place in the Palace Theatre and the crowd was to be drawn solely from amongst those men engaged in war work.

Mr Asquith was to follow up his speech by visiting the Scotswood works of Armstrong Whitworth's the next day. Mr Asquith's speech was positive in tone but was largely designed to appeal to the patriotism of the industrial working classes. The speech conveyed the sense that the Newcastle workers were valued by the country and that they were as much a part of the war effort as those fighting in the front lines. Most of the workers had time to change before the meeting and the majority wore suits and almost all proudly wore the small war service medal which marked them as 'industrial soldiers'. The Prime Minister stated the importance of Newcastle by declaring that there was nowhere else in the British Empire where the nation's fortune was so bound up with the efforts of the workers. The three main points included an appeal to firms to limit profits, to workers to restrict industrial action and trade union regulations that led to idleness, and, thirdly, to reassure firms that the government would be willing to offer compensation to those whose peacetime business suffered because of wartime demands.[47] Mr Asquith wisely avoided the subject of drunkenness which was a subject which continually irritated the workers and instead concentrated on the issue which most affected productiveness in Newcastle; the scarcity of skilled labour. Mr Asquith also denied that shortages of ammunition had crippled the operations of the army. The speech was warmly received, with cheers throughout, by the 4,000 workers who were present and during the tour of the munitions work the next day, accompanied by his wife, daughters, the Lord Mayor and Lady Mayoress, the Prime Minister was cheered by the workers in

Mr Asquith touring Newcastle after his speech: Daily Mirror, 22 April 1915.

the shell and fuse workshops. The speech met with a mixed reception in the national press however. *The Times*, in particular, was critical claiming that Mr Asquith had omitted a great deal and had been overly optimistic about the war.[48]

The committee acted quickly and asked all engineering, shipbuilding and repairing companies on the north-east coast to provide feedback on the numbers they employed, what they worked on and, in the case of those working on government contracts, their labour requirements. This information was to be used to ascertain the availability of skilled labour, the possibilities of sub-contracting important work and how many men it might be possible to transfer to required areas. In order to supply skilled labour to the Newcastle industries the committee considered the possibility of approaching the army to secure the release of many of the skilled munitions workers who had joined up at the start of the war while localised actions to limit the effect of alcohol were also considered.

The shortage of workers was particularly acute at Armstrong Whitworth's and the firm claimed that its Elswick works could employ another 2,000 skilled men and between 6 and 8,000 un-skilled workers. The labour exchanges diverted men from other districts such as textile machinery workers from Oldham but not all of these proved suitable. The increasing use of women in some tasks was, however, proving a success and was expanded.

As women became ever more prominent and were even recruited directly into their own branch of the Army ever more women found themselves attaining positions of great authority. Mrs Grimson became Recruiting Controller of the Women's Army Auxiliary Corps at Newcastle

The concerns over the production of munitions led to patriotic demonstrations and suggestions from the workers and a wide variety of Newcastle based groups. The Chamber of Commerce, for example, volunteered the services of over 100 of its members who had volunteered to work in their spare time from 6.00pm to midnight at the munitions works at Elswick. The offer, while demonstrating the patriotic fervour that was still in place amongst the middle classes in Newcastle, was regretfully turned down as it was necessary to keep the machines in the factory working round the clock and therefore it was only useful to employ men who could work a full shift.

By the end of April into May, the press and some areas of the government were still alleging that heavy drinking and high wages were responsible for declining productivity in shipbuilding with press coverage being particularly feverish. The Director of Naval Equipment, Captain Greatorex RN, made the rather panicked claim that the situation on the Tyne was so severe that production could come to a standstill and blamed this on the high Sunday wages (despite the fact that Sunday working was in decline) and the early opening of public houses in the vicinity of the yards (a measure which largely catered to those workers coming off nightshift rather than those going to work). The Home Office sent special investigators to a variety of shipbuilding areas with six visiting Tyneside. The reports of these investigators acknowledged that high wages were commonplace and that some workers were heavy drinkers but also blamed scarcity of labour and fatigue amongst the workers.

Although lack of shells had been a problem since 1914, the matter came to a head with the devastating report in *The Times* on 14 May which blamed the failure of the attack at Aubers Ridge during the offensive at Neuve-Chapelle on a lack of high-explosive shells. After receiving a deputation from the Conservative Party and after Lord Fisher's resignation Mr Asquith wrote to his ministers demanding their resignations and Asquith formed a new coalition government appointing David Lloyd George as Minister of Munitions. This resulted in the creation of new shadow munitions factories and in a campaign to rapidly increase the production of munitions. Thanks to the early establishment of the North-East Coast Armaments Committee Newcastle was able to react quickly.

It was not just shells which were proving problematic as naval losses became alarming in the Dardanelles an extraordinary meeting of the North-East Coast Armaments Committee met to discuss the possibility of setting up a flying column of armament workers who could move from yard to yard in order to advance the speed of completion of replacement ships and armaments. Over 1,000 delegates were present (representing over 150,000 men) along with members of the committee, the Lord Mayor and, the representative of the Admiralty Captain Power. The Admiralty declared that new and better ships were needed to replace the heavy losses suffered in the Dardanelles campaign and the mounting losses in the North Sea and that these ships must be completed as quickly as possible. He told the meeting that the King had asked him to express his concerns and to request that they do all that they could as it was an urgent situation. He went on to remind the men that the country was now being run on borrowed money and that they owed it to their colleagues fighting abroad not to make any further exorbitant demands for more wages. Continuing labour shortages were also discussed and this resulted in a mass campaign to recruit for the munitions industries with the labour exchange in Newcastle opening special offices for the purpose of recruitment.

After the government announced the policy of the dilution of skilled labour with semi and un-skilled labour in order to resolve the ongoing manpower shortages in the munitions industries the Minister of Munitions was keen to address the concerns of the workforce in Newcastle. He thus addressed a meeting of 900 trade union officials at Rutherford College in order to assuage their concerns. The munitions workers were extremely concerned over the threat presented by dilution and strongly resented the new measures as they believed that there were sufficient skilled men available if the government organized things properly. During the meeting Mr Lloyd George made a very urgent appeal for the workers to accept the measure and to co-operate in every way as it was the only way that sufficient manpower could be raised in order to produce munitions on the scale that they were needed. The press reported that the minister was well received and the meeting was closed with the members proposing and carrying a unanimous vote of thanks to Mr Lloyd George. However, this view was thrown into some doubt as it appears that certain sections of the workforce remained opposed to the measure regardless of what the trade union representatives might say.

Although the war created tying circumstances for many Newcastle businesses it also provided opportunities. The conversion of the lunatic asylum to a military hospital, for example, entailed a great many tenders. The majority of these were competed for and ultimately completed by local firms and involved many different trades. The first round of tenders, for example, included bedsteads, bedding, wardrobes, lockers, mirrors and doors. The major beneficiaries were Bainbridge & Co. who succeeded in bidding for contracts for beds, blankets and quilts with tenders worth £1,090 4 shillings 2 pence; and H. Chapman & Co. who were contracted to provide mattresses, pillows and lockers worth £900 12 shillings 6 pence.[49] Later tenders saw further opportunities for local businesses with items including building work, painting, the supply of groceries, tea, coal fish, ales and spirits, electric motors, blinds, cold room machinery and laundry machinery. Such business opportunities resulted in profits for Newcastle companies and are one example of how the wartime conditions actually aided some businesses.

The increasing success of the German submarines was resulting in worrying food shortages and the government was keen to increase the acreage of land used for agriculture and the efficiency of agricultural production. In Newcastle, the agricultural department of Armstrong College had turned its collective mind to increasing the use of new machinery on the land in order to improve efficiency and to free up more men for military service. At the end of August the college launched a series of exhibitions featuring new machinery including a new combined turnip thinner and horse hoe manufactured by a Darlington company.

In addition to the worries over supplies the increasing attacks by submarines also led to huge costs for Newcastle based ship-owners. The risks were clearly demonstrated by the ordeal suffered by the passengers and crew of the Prince Line steamer SS *Japanese Prince* in early December. The steamer, carrying cargo and a considerable number of passengers, was heavily shelled by an enemy submarine for over five hours as she tried to outrun the

Table i.
Tenders for Equipment and Work at Newcastle Lunatic Asylum (Northumberland No 1 War Hospital).

Item	Company	Notes
Bedsteads	Bainbridge & Co.	Market Street.
Blinds	ditto	
Blankets & Misc. Bedding	ditto	
Wash Stands	ditto	
Mirrored Wardrobes	W.E. Harker	Grainger Street.
Wardrobes	ditto	
Cold Store	Unknown	
Building Work	Mr Alex Pringle	
Lockers	Mr Alex Pringle	
Mattresses & Pillows	H. Chapman & Co.	Northumberland Street.
Pedestal Lockers	ditto	
Painting	A. Robertson	
Groceries	Thomas Worthington	
Bovril	Bovril Ltd.	
Tea & Coffee	Thomas Bell & Son Ltd.	Bath Lane
Butchers Meat	R.A. Dodds	Grainger Market
Poultry, Rabbits, Fish, etc	F.H. Phillips & Co.	
Milk	Carrick's Dairy Co.	Various locations in Newcastle.
Butter	Scandinavian Butter Co.	
Coal	W. Swallow & Co.	Gosforth, Newcastle.
Coal	Burradon & Coxlodge Coal Co.	
Coal	Seaton Burn Coal Co.	Akenside House, Akenside Hill, Newcastle
Electric Motors	Robson & Coleman	
Laundry Machinery	Isaac Braithwaite & Son	Kendal, Cumberland
Ales, Wines and Spirits	Unknown	

craft. Thanks to the efforts of captain and crew, the ship managed at last to shake off the submarine and make port with no casualties. For his efforts the skipper, Captain Jenkins, was awarded the sum of £500 by the directors of the company and a further £500 was distributed amongst the crew. Other rewards went to C. Hetherington, an apprentice, onboard the Newcastle steamer SS *Jacona*. When his ship was mined in the North Sea, Hetherington swam to an upturned lifeboat and after righting it rowed to the rescue of the rest of the crew and managed to rescue half of them. For his courage Hetherington was awarded a medal and diploma by Sir Walter Runciman.

It seems that many qualified professionals were already assisting in their free time by offering their expertise to military units in training. A letter from a Mr F.O. Hunt of Newcastle to *The Times* on 16 January, highlighted the success of one such scheme that had been instigated by Mr Hunt himself. As a qualified engineer and surveyor Mr Hunt had volunteered the use of his expertise in range-finding techniques to a local brigade of the Royal Field Artillery. His offer was accepted and he had dedicated the entirety of his free time to the training which had been highly successful. Mr Hunt wrote to the newspaper in order to publicize the scheme, to offer his services to other units, to appeal to other qualified professionals to offer their own services and to highlight the need for experienced instructors in the use of telephone equipment. In this manner, private citizens, many of whom were unlikely to ever be called up, could offer their services to the military and make a significant contribution to the war effort.

It was not only military men who received recognition for bravery, many mercantile marine men found themselves commended for bravery. This is Mr John William Bell of the Newcastle based SS Thordis. *The* Thordis *was responsible for the sinking of a German submarine: Daily Record, 5 March 1915.*

Notes

29 WAM: 374/10. *Wor Contemptible British Army and The Big Push*, c. 1916.

30 Priestley voices his opinions in his book *English Journey*. He was totally unimpressed by the northeast and this was exacerbated by his visits to the region during the depression.

31 Tyne & Wear Archives & Museums: MD.NC/141/4. Lunatic Asylum Visiting Committee; 8 April 1915, pp. 306.

32 Ibid, pp. 307-309.

33 The clerks were paid 35 shilling per week while the dispensers received £2 2 shillings per week.

34 TWAM: MD.NC/141/4. Lunatic Asylum Visitors Committee, 20 April - 4 May 1915, pp. 312-320.

35 Ibid, 4-13 May 1915, pp. 320-327.

36 Ibid, 6 July 1915 – 25 December 1915, pp. 342-381.

37 *New Zealand Herald*, Volume LII, Issue 15924, 22 May 1915, pp. 4.

38 *The Times*, 15 April 1915, pp. 10.

39 *The Times*, 20 January 1915, pp. 5.

40 Joannu. Paul: *United*.

41 *Newcastle Weekly Journal*, 14 May 1915, pp. 5.

42 Ibid, 18 August 1915, pp. 3.

43 Gregory. Adrian: *The Last Great War. British Society and the First World War* (2008), pp. 88.

44 *The Times*, 29 May 1915, pp. 8.

45 Ibid, 10 April 1915, pp. 5.

46 Ibid, 13 April 1915, pp. 5.

47 *The Spectator*, 24 April 1915, pp. 5.

48 *The Times*, 22 April 1915, pp. 11.

49 TWAM: MD.NC/141/4: Lunatic Asylum Visiting Committee, 13 April 1915, pp. 310-311.

CHAPTER 3

1916
The Realization

Since late 1915, the government had been well aware of the requirement for greater numbers within the army and as such the Military Service Act passed parliament on 4 January and would become law on 27 January. This act meant that every British resident aged 18 to 41 years-old who was single or who was a widower with no children or other dependents was considered to have enlisted for service in any unit. In Newcastle it was believed that the majority of people agreed with the act and, although compulsion was not widely liked, it was believed to be necessary to force young single men who had not volunteered to accept their obligation to their country. Not everyone supported the act and a meeting of the Independent Labour Party was held in Newcastle on 22 January with admission being by ticket. A large and hostile crowd, with many in uniform, assembled outside the hall and made an attempt to force their way into the building in order to disrupt the meeting but were held back by the stewards. The crowd instead retreated outside and held an impromptu meeting of their own during which they adopted resolutions in support of Lord Kitchener and the government. Towards the end of the meeting a large group of soldiers did succeed in forcing their way into the hall but behaved in an orderly manner and merely observed the proceedings and the meeting broke up quickly.

The scheme was quickly put into action and before men were called there had been a further surge of voluntary recruitment at Newcastle. Many of the men who had been holding back obviously deciding that, as they would be compelled anyway, they should volunteer. Others sought to escape compulsory service with some claiming that they were against the war for reasons of belief, that they were needed at their place of work, or that they were the main or sole providers for their families. In order to rule on these cases a local military tribunal was set up. The tribunal met regularly so, for example, in early June the tribunal discussed the cases of thirty-three men who were attested to serve under the Derby Scheme. The majority of these men were small tradesmen who claimed that if compelled they would lose their businesses. Of particular interest were two single young clerks (aged 23 and 27 years-old) from the Benwell, Scotswood, Elswick and Westgate tax office. Appearing before the tribunal on their behalf was their manager, Mr Freeman, who claimed that the men were vital as the office was working longer hours due to the numbers of additional munitions workers and that the office was responsible for collecting £250,000 in taxes. While the panel agreed that the work was of national importance it was not vital that young single men be employed to perform such work when they were needed at the front. The manager claimed that women had proven unsuitable for the job but was told that elsewhere women had proven themselves admirably suitable for such clerical positions. Mr Freeman then complained that the government would not pay extra to recruit more staff to replace already qualified workers but was told that it was his place to petition the government on this point and them men were given a two month exemption during which time the panel expected to see their positions taken over by women or ineligible men.

It seems clear that some young men in clerical positions who were eligible were being encouraged by their employers to go before the tribunal after being told that their positions were too important for them to be called up. This attitude contrasts strongly with the large numbers of clerical workers who had voluntarily enlisted during the first two years of the war. The remaining eligible men seem to have been split between those who were quite willing to serve but required reassurance that this would not ruin themselves or their family and those who clearly had no intention of being sent to the front if at all possible. A clear case of this seems to have come before the tribunal early in July (when the news of the fighting on the Somme had broken and the members of the tribunal were, perhaps, not overly prepared to be lenient) when a Newcastle based Scottish draper appealed on behalf of one of his salesmen who he claimed it would be improper to compel. The case revolved around the draper's sense of (perhaps Presbyterian) morality and the increasing role of women during the war. The man claimed that his business would suffer as the salesman was expected to measure clients and that this work would be impossible for a woman to undertake as it would mean her measuring men and that this would be indecent. Clearly the panel thought that the man was either a slacker or that his employer was merely seeking to protect his own business ahead of the national interest and totally refused the claim ordering that the man be immediately compelled.

As the fighting on the Somme went on the appeals tribunal clearly became firmer and less forgiving of those appearing before it. On 5 July, there were forty appeals before the panel and only one was upheld although several others received limited deferrals in order to put their affairs in order before compulsion.

The above cases do serve to again highlight the growing importance of women in the workplace. Although it was not altogether unheard of for some women to be employed in clerical roles the numbers increased dramatically during the war with large numbers of women undertaking office work in order to replace Newcastle men who had volunteered for service or subsequently been compelled. Many of these women were unskilled and, in order to function in their new roles, required training which some employers saw as an imposed burden. However, the majority of employers were delighted with how well the new workforce performed and there were many examples of employers offering praise to the women for their professionalism and dedication. The case of the draper's salesman also highlights a job which previously would not have been undertaken by a woman for, although most would probably not have been offended, reasons of propriety. Clearly the war was continuing to make inroads into traditional gender attitudes in Newcastle.

Despite the threat of compulsion it seems that a significant number of Newcastle men continued to come forward to volunteer for military service as recruiting offices maintained a steady flow of men. The news of the implementation of compulsion had also seen a burst of recruitment as had the news of losses at the Somme.

A People's War?

As the war dragged painfully into its third year, the people of Newcastle continued to back the war effort through fundraising activities and a marked willingness to invest in war bonds also to contribute to local, national and international charitable wartime causes. For the civilian population this was a means of feeling that they were aiding the men who were serving at the front and that they too were making sacrifices (if not in blood then monetary). It would seem that in Newcastle, as was common elsewhere, people had an idea of comparing scale of sacrifice to an economic model. The working class Newcastle labourer-poet Alfred Reeve expressed the idea of an economy of sacrifice in his 1916 poem *The Separation Allowance*:

The money is paid out, there is no eagerness.
Money for Mons!
Money for Neuve Chapelle, Loos, The Somme!
The banks of the universe could not meet the debt –
All the world's a creditor.

The soldier's wife enters a little city church
And the door folds her from the clang'rous city street
I peer through the dim light from sacred windows
As she kneels and prays
Hoping with her that he will come back

The world's a creditor
But if he does not return,
Heaven will pay the debt.[50]

The willingness of Newcastle's civilian population to advertise their sacrifice and contribution was clearly demonstrated by the popularity of the newly available National Service department pendant. The little heart-shaped medal was available only to those who could prove that their relative(s) were serving and cost 1 shilling. The popularity and purpose of the pendant was further demonstrated by the one word engraved on the front; Sacrifice. Many men who were working in engineering, munitions and shipbuilding wore the little silver medal which denoted that they were taking part in work vital to the war effort and the wearing of this crossed the classes with many young working men wearing these as they made it clear that they were not shirkers while bosses also wore the medal as it showed the contribution they were making. Indeed, the wearing of the medal by a number of managers was commented on by the King when he visited Tyneside.

The surge in orders for the armaments industries and the need to resolve the manpower shortages that affected production in Newcastle resulted in an influx of workers from outside the city and, as a consequence, living accommodation had become extremely scarce and that which was available was expensive. Newcastle was, and remains, a relatively compact city and the influx put unbearable pressure on already straining accommodation which was further compounded by the lack of new housing. Builders were suffering from the same manpower shortages and increased taxes alongside the availability of work on military and industrial contracts. The shortages had existed before the war but were now much more acute and made worse by the fact that speculative building on the part of building firms was unlikely due to the high costs of materials and limited number of available labourers while priority in accommodation had been given to housing the newly formed army units. In Newcastle the situation was further exacerbated by the lack of speculative building in previous years due to the imposition of new land taxes and by the start of the year there were no houses to let for below £50 per annum. Although Newcastle had a plan to build new housing at Walker this scheme had been delayed and the scarcity of adequate housing was now so severe that advertisements were appearing in local newspapers offering to £3 to any person who could enable the advertiser to secure three or four room flats.

The manpower shortages were somewhat eased by the influx of workers from elsewhere, by dilution of skilled labour and by the employment of more women. Some famous Newcastle businesses were badly affected by the war and many lost a number of former employees who had enlisted. Bainbridge's, for example, had twelve former employees killed in 1916 alone (from a total of twenty-seven former employees who were killed. These included the owners' son, Wilfred Hudson Bainbridge, who died of wounds in March while serving as adjutant to the 6th Battalion, Northumberland Fusiliers (Wilfred's older brother, Lieutenant Thomas Lindsay Bainbridge had been killed a year earlier at Ypres while commanding the Northumbrian Division Signalling Company). Many of the men who left Bainbridge's to join up were married and served in the 16th Battalion (Tyneside Commercials), Northumberland Fusiliers.

Dilution of labour was seen as essential by the government and was widely welcomed by management and by those who did not work within the affected industries. These people could not understand why many Newcastle workers saw dilution as an insult and a threat to their livelihoods. Many of the Newcastle workers remained hostile to, or at best suspicious of, the dilution of skilled labour. They believed that it undermined their own job security as it allowed management to hire less-skilled workers at a lower rate of pay. Demarcation of labour was prevalent in Tyneside's heavy industries and the workers were suspicious that the dilution of labour would be retained after the war in order to lower wage levels overall. For many of the workers there was a feeling of betrayal not only from their fellow citizens but also by their own unions. Although Newcastle workers remained incredibly loyal they were disgruntled by what they saw as a willing surrender of their skilled status and by the removal of their right to take strike action. It is clear, however, that the workers of Newcastle tended to accept dilution of labour more readily than their compatriots in other towns and cities. A possible explanation is that with a huge employer such as Armstrong Whitworth in the city workers were more likely to be passive but a more credible explanation seems to be that an equable settlement to the dilution issue had been reached. One of the keys to this settlement was that the numbers of female workers would be kept as low as possible and that the women's services would be dispensed with as soon as this was financially viable. The workers at Armstrong Whitworth's even had a clause built into their settlement which entitled them to full skilled rate pay without deduction for supervisions.[51] This is certainly the explanation for the low numbers of female workers in heavy industry in Newcastle when compared to other locations.

The increased employment and wages of the munitions workers led to some disharmony in Newcastle as old class-based prejudices resurfaced and widened traditional divisions between those employed in heavy manual labour and white-collar workers (many of whom had enlisted) and their families. Once again the root cause of this was a want to see an equality of sacrifice. Many of the families of men who had enlisted believed that they were making by far the greater sacrifice in terms of separation, worry and the possible loss or maiming of loved ones and these feelings were exacerbated by their being left in the city to witness what they perceived as the growing wealth of those workers who, they believed, were growing rich off the war. For those determined to find fault with the manual labourers and munitions workers there were easy targets. The most easily available target was to claim that the workers' moral standards, always suspect, had declined due to their increased earning.

It is undeniable that, although expected to work harder, those Newcastle residents who worked in the munitions industries were being paid at a higher rate than ever before. Much of the criticism they received from a number of groups over their use of the higher wages was based on the assumption that they were simply drinking the excess and that an orgy of drunkenness demonstrated that these wages were unsuitable and that the war effort was being directly affected by it.

Drinking in Newcastle was seriously affected by local and national measures which included a two-tier beer duty, the doubling of spirit duty and quadrupling of wine duty. The Central Control Board then made its presence felt when the chairman visited Newcastle and declared that he intended to make alcohol available only during two meal periods and to stop the practice of credit and treating (i.e. people buying drinks for others). All of these measures were intended to curtail drinking and create better order in Newcastle society. To an extent they succeeded and by 1916 the board was claiming that the restrictions had enabled 'better order in the streets, more comfortable homes, better cared for children, and better timekeeping at work.'[52]

The restrictions had a severe effect on the extensive brewing industry in Newcastle. Many firms restricted the number of beers they produced, reduced the strength of those they did continue to produce and cut back on supply, especially to the clubs. The clubs and their members were distinctly aggrieved at these measures and many meetings were held to protest against them. The clubs were a home to a broad cross section of Newcastle society with some being overtly political in nature (e.g. the Elswick Conservative Workingmen's Club), nationalist and political (the Irish Literary Institute), work ties (the Tramway & Vehicle Workers Social Club, the Elswick Collieries Workingmen's Social Club) and sports groups with licensed clubhouses. Newcastle even had a Catholic club which had received a blessing from the Pope.[53]

Newcastle also had a number of gentlemen's clubs although most of these were long established. Newer clubs had received a bad press in Newcastle before and during the war with several being closed for allowing excessive drunkenness (e.g. the Blackett Club) or for tolerating misbehaviour of various degrees. Even the patriotically inclined clubs were not immune as was made clear by the expulsion of the United Services Club during the war.

The increased regulations, limited brewing and price rises led to rising protests with the Workmen's Protection League taking up the battle behind the slogan 'Give Us Beer and Regular Hours'. Industrial unrest was actually aggravated by the shortage of supplies of drink and by the prohibitive costs. A common theme in the daily and weekly correspondence columns of local newspapers was the poor quality of the drink being served in Newcastle. Brewers were blamed amidst claims that they were selling poor quality products and vastly overpricing them.

Clearly the continuous and at times hostile debate which raged around alcohol consumption on Tyneside also highlighted the class and social divisions within the city. The upper and managerial classes, including the Shipbuilding Employers' Federation, campaigned throughout the war for a total ban on alcohol while at times demonizing the men who were working ever longer hours for them at greatly increased profitability.

Others, more outwardly charitable but still patronisingly ignorant, were despairing of what they saw as the waste of money due to these workers having previously impossible levels of money available to them. One Newcastle gentleman was moved to write to *The Times*, exhorting the government to do something about this which would benefit both the workers themselves and the war effort. Mr Frederic C. Coley stated that a scheme selling war bonds and/or savings certificates should be instigated within the pay offices of all the munitions works and that this would enable the men (there is no reference to the women who were working) to save up to £1 per week for after the war. Mr Coley was rightly concerned that the munitions workers would never again be paid at the level they were and that they should therefore think of their future and put some money aside. However, he also demonstrates a lack of understanding of the working classes and assumes that if this is not enacted then the working man would simply find the extra money burning a hole in his pocket and would fritter it away. There is no acknowledgement of the fact that although wages had increased dramatically so had living expenses and many families were still struggling to survive. Once again this shows the difference in attitudes and lack of empathy which still marked the class differences in wartime Newcastle society.

Indeed, the workers of the Newcastle munitions industries made significant voluntary contributions to a large number of wartime charities demonstrating a commitment to the war effort and a sober dedication which is at odds with the description of them as spending their increased wages largely on drink. From the first month of 1915 to mid 1916 they had collectively donated over £24,000 to the Lord Mayor's Fund, £2,080 to the Prince of Wales' Fund and goods worth over £2,000. In total, the munitions workers had contributed at least £36,630 alongside untallied contributions towards gifts for soldiers and 1,300,000 cigarettes for the front. Such was the enthusiasm for supporting the armed forces that the workers of the Small Shell Works Department, Deleval Works, Scotswood, organized a day out in the country for wounded and disabled soldiers. Clearly it was an insult to these men to imply that en-masse they were squandering their increased earnings on drink and other unwholesome and unpatriotic frivolities.

For the women of Newcastle the war brought worry, hardship and, in some cases limited opportunity. We have already seen how Newcastle women were eager to join the workforce in industries which previously had not employed women but women also gained opportunities for employment in other areas.

The war offered many new opportunities for Newcastle women. Here are conductresses at Wingrove Depot in 1915. (Newcastle City Library)

The extensive tram network was labour dependant and large numbers of employees had joined up at the start of the war meaning that there were significant shortages. While driving was still seen as a specialist job, for men only, the role of conductor was made available for women who proved to excel in the job and by 1916 there were a significant number of conductresses around Newcastle.

In general, from immediately pre-war, the price of staple foods had increased by 48 per cent by March.[54] Prices continued to rise and by October the Board of Trade conceded that the prices of principle foodstuffs had increased by 65 per cent from July 1914. The steadily increasing prices of food resulted in queuing at Newcastle shops and, despite the increased level of wages in some industries, resulted in hardships for many Newcastle families. The most seriously affected were those who had men who they had depended upon who were in the armed forces overseas or had already been killed or seriously injured. For these unlucky families the incoming wages had failed to keep pace with the higher cost of living and it was a real

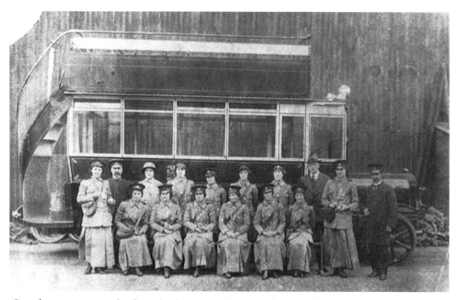

Conductresses worked on the buses in Newcastle too! This wartime photograph shows uniformed conductresses and three male workers in front of an open topped double-decker. (Newcastle City Library)

struggle to put food on the table. Quite obviously the situation could not go on and in November the Board of Trade gained powers to stop wastage, control manufacture and production of many items, control the markets and regulate prices of staple foodstuffs.

Even during the height of fighting in 1916, there was still an attempt by the businesses and press of Newcastle to maintain a business as usual attitude with extensive adverts for the summer sales appearing in local newspapers next to news from the Somme frontline. Fenwick's and Bainbridge's in particular had large adverts repeatedly throughout the first week of the battle. Other signs of some semblance of normality could be seen in the reporting of popular entertainment with music halls and theatres remaining popular, being described as busy all day, and the Tyne Theatre urging people to take the last opportunity to see the film *The Birth of a Nation* during the last scheduled week of showing. It was claimed that the film had been extremely popular in attracting large crowds and that there was widespread interest on Tyneside.

Sport also continued to be a popular recreation for those who could afford it. On the same day as soldiers were going over the top on the Somme the Newcastle United Golf Club was reporting the results of its Calcutta Cup match between the eventual winner George Little and runner-up, Thomas Chisholm, to an eager response on the local press.

Given that Newcastle was so vital to the nation's munitions production it was only natural that the residents would take an exceptional pride in the value of their work. The shipyard workers keenly followed the exploits of the Royal Navy and, in particular, the fortunes of the ships that they had themselves produced on the Tyne. Early in the war they had been encouraged by the press to take pride in the vessels that they had constructed which were now protecting Britain through service with the Grand Fleet. This pride could of course be a double edged sword and the first news of the Battle of Jutland came as something of a shock to many on Tyneside. Just days after the battle (31 May – 1 June) it became clear that heavy losses had been suffered and it is evident that the local press, along with the local authorities, did not quite know how to report the news of the battle. The Lord Mayor was forced to give a statement declaring that the true result was not yet known but that there was certainly no reason to be ashamed of 'our Jack Tars'. Clearly the local authorities were anxious over the effect news of losses could have on the morale of the munitions workers and were determined to put on as brave a face as possible.[55] Of the fourteen RN ships sunk during the battle, five had been built on the Tyne including two of the three battle cruisers (HMS *Queen Mary* at Palmers and HMS *Invincible* at Armstrong Whitworth; other losses were the destroyers HMS *Shark* and HMS *Sparrowhawk* (Swan Hunter & Wigham Richardson) and HMS *Turbulent* (Hawthorn Leslie)). The loss of these ships hit morale on Tyneside hard. So severe was the effect that the local press even reported that the loss of HMS *Queen Mary* in particular had been very keenly felt.

Although morale remained generally high at Newcastle it was prone to being effected negatively by events which outwardly had no connection with Tyneside. For example, morale was adversely affected by the death of Lord Kitchener on 5 June. Kitchener was drowned after the ship he was on, HMS *Hampshire*, was sunk by a mine off the Orkney Islands en-route to Russia. In marked comparison to other northern English towns (*The Manchester Guardian* reporting that it was a blessing as Kitchener had been a liability) the loss of Kitchener appears to have been widely and genuinely mourned and regretted by the people of Newcastle. Letters of condolence appeared in local newspapers and speeches of commemoration were made including that which was roundly applauded at Byker which stated that Kitchener's death was, 'probably the greatest blow that this country had received since the war began.'[56]

The normally steady morale was also affected by the news of the fighting on the Somme battlefields. Although the local and national press put a positive accent on the news of the battle with daily positive reports these were counterbalanced by the loss lists published daily which clearly demonstrated the huge scale of the losses to the British Army. The *Evening Chronicle*, for example, ran a story on the evening of first day of the battle claiming that the British attack had been successful.[57] Continuing in the same vein the people of Newcastle were told on 3 July, that the German lines had been broken and that the news of the battle was overwhelmingly positive. Almost a week after the commencement of the battle the local press, largely using stories culled from national sources, were printing extremely positive, and inaccurate, stories about the battle with a strong leaning towards the dramatic with headlines such as 'The Dash Across No-Mans' Land' being prominent.[58]

Juxtaposed, sometimes on the same page, with ever-increasing casualty lists this news must have made painful and bewildering reading for many a Newcastle resident but was clearly designed to maintain morale amongst the civilian population, many of whom still knew very little of actual conditions at the front. Indeed, tensions over the position of many young men could and were boiling over in Newcastle, as elsewhere. There was anger directed at some young men who were seen out and about in civilian clothing as it was assumed, often incorrectly, that they were slackers and shirkers who had little intention of serving or helping the country. The situation had obviously become more marked in the aftermath of the Somme as one former Sergeant was moved to write to the local newspapers urging people to 'refrain from scowls and snubs' aimed at such men as many of them, like himself, had suffered wounds, including the loss of limbs, and had been discharged by the army as being unfit for further duty. These men had served their country and did not deserve the ridicule which some residents were inflicting upon them.

The Somme

Although most people think of the dreadful casualties suffered on the first day of the battle the men of Newcastle raised battalions were in action in the days leading up to the battle. On the night of 21 May, 'D' Company of the 25th (2nd 'Tyneside Irish') Battalion was holding the line on the right of their Brigade position in front of La Boiselle when a German raiding party attacked a post held by a six man section. The battalion war diary lists three men being killed with a further three wounded while 25/290 Lance Corporal Thomas Hilton repelled the attack by with hand grenades. A year later in July 1917,

Hilton was awarded the Military Medal largely for this action.[59] Amongst the fatalities listed for this date are Second Lieutenant William Leonard Hopps who died of wounds on the 22nd, 26 year-old Lance Corporal John Armstrong of Derwenthaugh (21 May 1916), Private James Brennan of Gateshead (22 May 1916), and Private Joseph K. Summers of Gateshead (22 May 1916). In the following days the Tynesiders launched their own raids; without a great deal of success and suffering further casualties. One of the raiding parties of the 24th Battalion (1st 'Tyneside Irish') was ambushed on reaching then enemy line and suffered two men injured. One of the men was carried back by an officer and by Newcastle-born Private Edmund Hedley who was aged just 19 years-old at the time and had developed a poor reputation for absenteeism while in training but was proving to be a good soldier on active service. Sadly, Private Hedley was killed on the Somme on 29 August 1917 leaving his young widow, Dorothy, to grieve back home in Newcastle. On the same night a raid mounted by the 26th (3rd 'Tyneside Irish') failed and came under heavy fire after being forced to retreat. The survivors were only able to escape back to friendly lines after another Newcastle native, Private John Clark, threw bombs and gave covering fire before he helped those who had been wounded back to the British lines.[60]

Among the pals battalions with strong connections to Newcastle which were facing action on the first day of the battle was the 16th (Newcastle) Battalion, Northumberland Fusiliers, which was commonly known as the 'Tyneside Commercials'. The 16th was a part of the 96th Brigade which consisted of three pals battalions (15th Lancashire Fusiliers (1st 'Salford Pals'), 16th Lancashire Fusiliers (2nd 'Salford Pals') and the 16th (Newcastle) Northumberland Fusiliers). The brigade had been given one of the most crucial and difficult tasks of the opening day; a direct attack upon the heavily fortified village of Thiepval. The attack was a disaster with heavy machine-gun fire causing very heavy casualties to the attacking battalions. In the case of the 16th (Newcastle) their trench system was even overlooked by the German machine gunners and the men of the 'Tyneside Commercials' never even made it to the German lines; many never even made it out of their own front line.

It was rumoured that the battalion, which contained a large number of very fine Tyneside sportsmen, launched the attack by kicking a ball ahead of them (either rugby or football, the accounts are not specific). After moving up to the trenches on the night of 30 June the battalion began taking casualties before it even reached its starting position. This was due to extremely heavy German artillery fire which continued throughout the night as the battalion stood-to. When moving off the leading companies were decimated by heavy and accurate machine-gun and rifle fire from the enemy trenches which overlooked the 16th's position. The enemy even stood on his parapet firing and urging the men of the battalion to 'come on'. The fire was so heavy that the leading companies were forced to take cover and when C Company, which was in support, attempted to move out of the trenches they too suffered very heavy casualties. So heavy were the casualties that the reserve company (D) and the battalion HQ moved up to offer further support but the first platoon over the top was mown down and the order given to instead man the parapet and give covering fire to enable the men of the first three companies to retreat.

By early morning, the company commanders of A and B companies had been killed and casualties continued to mount due in part to the refusal of command to allow a withdrawal as unsuccessful attempts were made to regain the initiative. Eventually the order to fall back was received. By the end of the day, the 16th Battalion had lost six officers killed along with over 350 NCO's and other ranks that had fallen. The next morning only eight officers and 300 other ranks answered roll call. The total casualties numbered thirteen officers and 365 other ranks. In addition to the two company commander's, officer casualties included Lieutenant Robert Whitfield Falconer of 3 Roseworth Terrace, Gosforth. Falconer had been a bell-ringer at All Saints' Church in Gosforth and is commemorated by a plaque in the church, a memorial to bell-ringers in Newcastle St Nicholas' Cathedral and in a list of bell-ringers from the north of England from a roll of honour held at St Paul's Cathedral. Lieutenant Falconer had left money for two new bells to be donated to All Saints in his will. As the official history of the battalion comments, 'The 'First of July' was a sad day for Tyneside; so many of her best and bravest went then to their last noble sleep.'[61]

Among those lost serving with the 'Tyneside Commercials' on the first day were two players who had represented Newcastle United Football Club before the war: 22 year-old Private Thomas Goodwill of Bates Cottages, Seaton Deleval, who was a senior Newcastle United player (an outside right); and 26 year-old Corporal Dan Dunglinson of the Esplanade (his elder brother, William was killed in 1918), Whitley Bay. Both men have no known grave and are commemorated on the Thiepval Memorial and the plaque at St James' Park.

Bainbridge's, the famous Newcastle department store, lost five former employees on the first day of the battle; all serving with the 'Tyneside Commercials'. The five were: Sergeant Henry Ernest Armstrong aged 24; Corporal James Ballantyne aged 22; Lance Corporal Charles Smith; Private

Ralph Edward Green aged 23; and Private Richard Nunn aged 21. All of these men have no known grave and all are commemorated on the Thiepval Memorial; the firm lost three other former employees in July (two from the 'Tyneside Commercials' and one serving with the Lancashire Fusiliers) with only one having a marked grave.

The Somme was also to prove fatal for another former Newcastle United player; Donald Simpson Bell was serving as a Second Lieutenant with the 9th Battalion of the Yorkshire Regiment and was killed on 10 July. Just five days previously, he had been awarded the Victoria Cross for charging over open ground under very heavy fire to eliminate an enemy machine gun which was holding up an advance. The official citation in *The London Gazette* declared, 'This very brave act saved many lives and ensured the success of the attack. Five days later, this very gallant officer lost his life performing a very similar act of bravery.'[62] Other men with Newcastle United connections killed during the year included former reserve player George Rivers, while former goalkeeper Thomas Richardson was killed on 15 September aged 36 years-old while serving with the 4th Battalion of the Yorkshire Regiment; he had been awarded the Military Cross earlier in the war.

For the 'Tyneside Irish' the battle began badly with two men, Private F. J. (John) Pepper of Durham and Private Joseph Messenger Armstrong of Penrith, of 'A' company of 24th Battalion (1st 'Tyneside Irish') killed and eleven injured in an accidental explosion as they collected bombs from an ammunition dump on their way to the Line late on the night of 30 June. In order to avoid the men losing heart and because it was thought unlucky before an attack, the bodies were taken to a nearby casualty clearing station where they lie buried (at Heilly Station Cemetery) to this day. Sadly, all too many of their comrades would shortly be joining the unfortunate two men.

The commanding officer of the 34 the division had placed the 103rd ('Tyneside Irish') Brigade in reserve ready to back up the initial attack with the 101st Brigade and the 102nd (Tyneside Scottish) Brigade would lead the attack. The plan, which involved the initial brigades advancing in columns while the 'Tyneside Irish' advanced in line abreast, was a remarkably unimaginative one which had several glaring weaknesses. The battalions crowded each other and had little room to manoeuvre in the event of them coming under heavy fire while Major-General Ingouville-Williams had also decided that the commanding officers and their headquarters staff would advance with their units. This meant that they were often killed and even the survivors had little perspective and could not make command decisions or reorganize the units if they suffered badly. Furthermore, the attack was expected as the Germans had intercepted a communication sent from either the Tyneside Scottish Brigade HQ which confirmed the attack would take place that morning. In his excellent account of the 'Tyneside Irish', John Sheen states that the blame for much of what followed attached to the 'Corps and Army commanders who ordered the men to advance in such a stupid formation over open ground'. Although I largely agree with this, it must be said that this and other similar claims are made with the benefit of hindsight and fail to take into account the belief of commanders that the unprecedented preparatory artillery barrage had destroyed both wire and enemy forces.

The men of the Tyneside Scottish Brigade waited impatiently for the detonation of the two huge mines that would signal the attack but discovered that once they had set off the artillery barrage had not been as effective as hoped and they were faced with narrow gaps in the barbed wire which funnelled them and made them even easier targets for the waiting German machine gunners. The brigade was accompanied from its 'jumping-off' positions by unarmed pipers; an unnamed officer believed to be from the Middlesex Regiment commenting, 'The pluckiest thing I ever saw was a piper of the Tyneside Scottish playing his company over the parapet.'[63] A number of the pipers paid the ultimate price including Lance Corporal Garnet Wolsley Fyfe of the 20th Battalion (1st Tyneside Scottish) who was described as being riddled by bullets during the advance across no-mans land. A piper of the 21st Battalion (2nd Tyneside Scottish), Private William Alexander Scott of Elswick, was killed in the enemy front-line trench with his pipes still in his hands. A fellow piper, George Griffiths, who witnessed the actions of his comrade during the advance claimed, 'If ever a man deserved the VC, Willie did'.[64]

The men of the Tyneside Scottish were mown down as they came down a slope and suffered very heavy casualties. On the left side of the brigade the 20th and 23rd Battalions pressed forward even though they had over 800yd to cross and had been under fire since the very start of the advance. A large number of these men successfully reached the German second line but were then wiped out while an attempt to take the village of La Boisselle. Once more the casualties suffered by officers as they tried to lead from the front and rally their men were appalling. In the 20th Battalion every officer became a casualty. So concentrated was the machine-gun fire that many men fell before crossing their own lines including the company commanders of both 'A' and 'B' companies of the 23rd Battalion.

Despite the severe casualties, men of the 22nd and 23rd Battalions also reached the second line of the enemy before setting off for the third line of trenches. The attack came under heavy fire and was unsupported due to the casualties that had been suffered and the men were forced to retreat.

Again, command and control deteriorated and it took some time for the picture to become clear to commanders behind the lines. When the news of the Tyneside Scottish Brigade did come through it was disastrous. To all extents two battalions (20th and 23rd), half of the brigade, had been annihilated while the other two battalions had managed to hold onto some territory but at the expense of terrible casualties. Furthermore, the land gained was now dangerously exposed on the flanks and the situation was only saved by the arrival of Major Acklom to take over command; this remnant, consisting of fewer than 200 men, held out before being reinforced and eventually they were relieved on 3 July.

The Tyneside Scottish had suffered some of the greatest casualties of any attacking brigade and although exact figures are hard to interpret it seems that the brigade lost between 2,288 and 2,438 officers and men killed, missing or wounded on 1 July. The dead included all four battalion commanders while every officer and sergeant of the 20th Battalion became casualties and of the 23rd Battalion only 100 men answered roll-call on the following day.

For the 'Tyneside Irish' Brigade their formation and position in reserve meant that they came under a heavy German barrage and suffered very heavily. Although the 'Tyneside Irish' suffered horrendous casualties during the advance, the courage of the largely untried men has been well attested to. Another Newcastle man, CQMS John Connolly of the 24th Battalion afterwards wrote home to his wife, Marion, praising the courage of the men even though many of the officers and senior NCO's were injured or killed early in the advance. Connelly was himself wounded and lost a leg; on 2 February 1918 he died as a result of his injuries aged 49 years-old, and is buried at Byker and Heaton Cemetery in Newcastle.

Officer casualties were extremely heavy; of four battalion commanders only one was unwounded while of the sixteen company commanders fifteen were casualties. Lieutenant Colonel Steward who had started the day in command of the 27th Battalion (4th 'Tyneside Irish') was summoned back to take command of the brigade. Unfortunately, by the time he returned to the lines the brigade had suffered such casualties that command and control, even reorganization, was all but impossible.

Advancing with the 'Tyneside Irish' that morning was one of those who had signed up while under-age. Private James Gillespie was only 15 years-old when he joined up in December 1914 after running away from home. Gillespie was originally from Kelso but his parents had moved to Newcastle before the beginning of the war. After the war he described his part in the first day of the battle to his sons. Gillespie served as runner to the adjutant of the 26th Battalion. When the adjutant was wounded during the uphill advance the RSM attracted Gillespie's attention, but before he could help the officer he was himself blown into a shell hole by an artillery round which knocked him unconscious and left him wounded in the neck and mouth. After regaining consciousness, Gillespie was sniped at and the lay still until he was rescued by a sergeant from a different regiment. On his way to being evacuated he discovered that all of his belongings, including his watch, money and wallet had been stolen. While Gillespie was in hospital, his age was discovered and he was discharged from the army returning to work as a miner. However, he was called up during the crisis of March 1918 and posted to France where he was again wounded. Again, he was discharged but immediately upon his recovery he joined The King's Own Scottish Borderers and served in India.[65]

The attack of the 25th and 26th Battalions was halted by the heavy fire and then forced to retreat back to friendly lines. Small groups from a number of battalions, mainly the 24th Battalion, had reached the German lines and had occupied the 'Lochnagar Crater' before pushing forward again. Some men of the 27th Battalion also kept going forward and dug in at 'Round Wood'. By this stage the attack had broken down completely with units hopelessly intermingled and the lack of officers led to a breakdown in organization. Although the picture was very confused, by noon it had become obvious that the attack had been a disaster.

Once again the exact casualty figures are extremely hard to confirm as many men died later of their injuries and some of those reported missing later turned up. However, the 'Tyneside Irish' Brigade is estimated to have lost somewhere in the region of 2,171 men killed, missing or wounded. Of the men lost on 1 July while serving with the Tyneside Brigades, a large proportion would never be found or identified and would therefore have no known grave. A large number are commemorated on the Thiepval Memorial to the missing. This commemorates 73,412 men with no known graves killed between 1916 and 1918. In terms of numbers the most numerous are Northumberland Fusiliers (2,931 in total or almost 4 per cent) with 590 other ranks being from the 'Tyneside Scottish' and 514 from the 'Tyneside Irish'. As Sheen points out this means that the Tyneside Battalions make up a very substantial 37.6 per cent of all Northumberland Fusiliers commemorated at Thiepval. However, it appears that the 87.7 per cent of 'Tyneside Irish' who died on 1 July was buried in unmarked graves. Once again Sheen appears to provide one possible answer to the question of why this might be so. As many of the men were coalminers, they were used to having tokens attached to their braces used to identify who had filled a particular tub of coal. The identity discs issued to them by the army were very similar to these tokens and therefore many men attached them to their braces rather than being worn around the neck as was standard practice. When a burial party opened a man's collar to identify him they could find no disc and thus the man was buried as an unknown soldier.[66] It would seem that this also applied to many other soldiers from the Northumberland and Durham coalfields.

Because of the nature of recruitment in the Kitchener battalions of Newcastle the first day of the Somme was by far and away the worst in terms of casualties for the city. When the extent of the casualties became known there was initially consternation on Tyneside as it became obvious that the men of the city had suffered massively during the battle. For the 'Tyneside Irish' and 'Tyneside Scottish' Brigades the first day of the attack had been an absolute disaster and the two formations were never the same again as from now on the Tyneside element was diluted by replacements posted in from various locations. The 'Tyneside Commercials' had also suffered huge losses and this had a 'knock-on' effect in Newcastle as most of the men were in similar professions and belonged to similar clubs and associations. Tragically, a large percentage of the men in the battalion were also married and so Newcastle was left with a large number of widows and orphaned children. Many of the companies and organization to which these men belonged attempted to alleviate the suffering of those left behind by making collections and setting up funds in order to provide some extra money for those who had lost their primary provider.

Industry

The loss of foreign trade continued to provide new opportunities for Newcastle-based manufacturers. In pre-war years the majority of leather gloves were imported from Germany and Austria as well as a more limited number from Australia and Canada. By 1916, the North of England Chamois Company, which had a substantial interest in the manufacturing of leather goods turned to glove making. This new industry required the recruitment of glove cutters from Somerset and also employed women and girls in their own homes in the stitching of the gloves. The women were in the main from the Spital Tongues area and scores were employed earning from 18 to 26 shillings per week. The gloves were then returned to the workshop for finishing before sale to large drapery companies in Newcastle, Northumberland and Durham. Shortages of trained workers remained a major hindrance to sales and the company estimated that it was only able to fulfil 10 per cent of the demand. To rectify this it had plans to train 500 women in the stitching operation.

Newcastle remained, in the third year of war, a diverse industrial area with a large number of widely differing manufacturers and merchants being based in the city. Clearly a large number of these were supplying materials for the main industries of shipbuilding, munitions, engineering and coal export. A quick glance through the entries for the city in *Wards' Directory* of 1915-1916 demonstrates this clearly. The coal industry, for example, has 165 separately listed coal merchants and a further seventy-three coal owners based in the city. In engineering, there are ninety-one companies listed but there are a number of these which were dependent on engineering, shipbuilding and/or munitions production for their livelihoods and several which could legitimately have been listed under the title of engineers themselves.

Criticism of workers for absenteeism continued in some quarters but these were becoming somewhat more muted as it became increasingly clear that the workers of Newcastle were doing an exceptionally important job and were doing it, by and large, very well with little political agitation or disruption. However, for some workers there were reasons to complain, and in late July the railway workers of Tyneside met at the Palace Theatre in order to demand a pay rise. The workers had a legitimate claim in that they had seen increases in wages for munitions workers but little or none for themselves even though they were also engaged in vital work which required long hours and often dangerous conditions. The workers claimed that they had no wish to profit from the war but that they needed the increase because the rise in the cost of living, notably food costs, had made it impossible for them to carry on supporting their families on pre-war wages.

For the ship owners of Newcastle the war was making business increasingly complicated and risky. Many were concerning themselves with the confusion that had affected their trade in recent months. The Admiralty had set up a number of committees which had an influence on the shipping of freight and it was believed that these committees were disjointed and acted in an uncoordinated manner which harmed the industry and the war effort. The owners were also complaining to the government over the amount of luxuries which were still being shipped at this time of national emergency and about the haphazard requisitioning of some shipping which was taking place. They argued that state hire of ships could be made to work but only if the ships were left under the control of their owners. The owners were given backing in this matter from the Chamber of Commerce and its president, Lord Joicey.[67] Between just three Newcastle-based companies (Prince Line, W. Runciman & Co, Sutherland Steam Ship Co.) the government had requisitioned twenty-six vessels from a total owned of eighty (32.5 per cent); Walter Runciman & Co. had lost almost 50 per cent of its fleet to government control.

Sir Walter outlined his concerns at the annual meeting of the Moor Line which he had founded. He argued that the independently owned fleets had more than proven their worth to the war effort and that each vessel that was requisitioned by the government forced the prices of shipping up even further and that this had the knock-on effect of increasing the cost of living for the people of Britain and increased the risk of a financial collapse which would destroy the war effort. He went on to hit back at those critics who were denouncing the independent fleet owners for charging excess fees by stating that this was only because they were suffering the loss of ships to ineffective government control, enemy action and increased insurance costs.

As if to highlight the risk facing those who were employed by these companies it was announced that a large steamer of the Prince Line, SS *Saxon Prince*, had been captured and sunk en-route from New Orleans to Great Britain by the German cruiser, SMS *Möwe*, with the entire crew being taken prisoner (ironically an identically named mine-sweeping trawler formerly of the North Shields fleet was sunk just a month later). The *Saxon Prince* was one of fifteen steamers sunk or captured by the German ship during this cruise in addition to the sinking of the battleship HMS *King Edward VII* by mines laid by the *Möwe*. With the increasing effectiveness of German submarine warfare, the mining of British waters and the risk of raiders the ship-owning companies of Newcastle were facing catastrophe, the possibility of losing ships on two fronts; government control and enemy action. It was to an extent countered by the greater prices being offered for cargoes but other costs included increasing insurance payments and wages.

However, the increasing number of merchant vessels that were being sunk resulted in large orders for some of the Newcastle-based shipbuilders as the government was urging these losses to the country's mercantile fleet to be replaced as quickly as possible. For example, Swan, Hunter & Wigham Richardson and also Palmer's received orders in early March for the building of two large steamers and the companies were in negotiations with several other fleet owners for the possible building of others.

The disruption caused to local business due to the loss of skilled labour to the army was a continuing source of comment in Newcastle. Annual meetings of various businesses repeatedly comment on these problems and proudly log the names and number of men who had fallen in the service of the nation. Broomhill Collieries Ltd, for example, held their annual meeting at Collingwood Buildings in October 1916 and stated that sixty of their former miners had been killed in action as had two of their Newcastle-based clerks and also several directors had lost sons in the fighting. While the loss of men did have an impact upon these businesses it seems that the majority of companies found ways of managing their manpower problems through a mixture of dilution of labour, longer working hours and increasing wages.

As ever, the key workers at Newcastle were seen to be those directly involved in the manufacture of munitions and a variety of methods were used to ensure that morale remained as high as possible and that the workforce were encouraged to take an interest in the war and to maintain and improve their efforts. Probably the most cynical of these methods was the use of (often spurious) interviews with serving soldiers who encouraged the men to greater efforts amidst encouragement and reproach. A typically clumsy attempt was published in The *Newcastle Evening Chronicle* on 1 August. The article purported to be from an interview with an unnamed infantry officer who was serving with a battalion at the front and included the following quote: 'If I were a munition [sic] worker, I think I'd feel I was doing as big a thing as anybody can do in this war. Time lost in munition [sic] production would seem to me a bit too much like murder. Holidays! Believe me, there isn't a munition [sic] worker in the country who'd take a holiday [even] if they were given treble pay for it; not if they could see just what the rising tide of guns and shells means to Tommy – and what even the slightest ebb would mean.' Clearly this article was written with the purposes of discouraging munitions workers to take holidays (to which they were entitled due to the arduous nature of their work), and to imply that Newcastle's munitions workers should not lose time as their absenteeism would directly lead to the deaths of British soldiers. The article used the typical carrot and stick approach by encouraging the workers to feel valued and a successful part of the war effort but that if they lessened their efforts they would be guilty of murdering British soldiers at the front.[68]

Other forms of encouragement to the munitions workers included the continuation of visits by delegates and VIP's. Among those in 1916, was a visit by two French soldiers (accompanied by an interpreter) to the various Tyneside works. The two were a curious choice: Lieutenant Weill, an officer with the 81st Infantry Division, had been an elected member of the German Reichstag representing the Social Democrats of Metz and was condemned to death for siding with France in the war; his companion, Private Cabanne, served with the 101st Regiment of French Artillery and was formerly organizer of the French United Socialist Party. Clearly the visitors had been handpicked to appeal to the working-class nature of the Tyneside munitions workers but it is interesting that one of them at least would also have had first-hand experience of using artillery pieces similar to those being manufactured on Tyneside. The visit was well received by the workers and the translated speeches warmly applauded and cheered.

Throughout 1916, the workers of Newcastle continued to show a determined resolution towards the war effort despite some well-publicised knocks. Although some employers still complained of absenteeism and drunkenness, these complaints had become more muted in tone and more realistic in context. The workers themselves had shown a willingness to undertake longer hours and to accept the dilution of labour, albeit with advantageous terms and conditions, and to show a marked reluctance to take illegal strike action when compared to other parts of the country. The reasons for this were many and varied ranging from the promise offered by increased wages, patriotism, and a personal connection to someone in the armed forces and the awareness of the importance of the work they were doing.

Zeppelins

On the night of 2/3 April, Newcastle was once again attacked by a Zeppelin. The German press subsequently claimed that wharves, buildings, blast furnaces and factories on the river were bombarded resulting in large explosions and the collapse of numerous buildings while an anti-aircraft battery was also bombed and silenced; the reports went on to describe how numbers of Newcastle factories shipyards were destroyed and the Tyne Bridge almost completely demolished. In actual fact, some four airships had set off to bomb targets in the Firth of Forth. Several managed to drop bombs on Edinburgh after failing to locate their targets while the L16 made landfall north of Blyth before turning south and dropping bombs seemingly at random (including on Cramlington) before turning back out to sea. The L22 made landfall near Berwick and dropped some bombs in that area before turning north to drop more bombs on Edinburgh. On his return to Germany, the commander (*Kapitanleutnant* Dietrich) claimed that he had bombed several factories in Newcastle (having apparently mistaken Berwick for the city or not being willing to own up to his error).[69]

During the period, Zeppelin raids had a significant effect on civilian morale and led many to question why more was not being done to protect the country from aerial attack. These concerns grew so great that questions were asked in the House of Commons and some MPs began campaigning energetically for an expansion of the air services (organized at the time into the Royal Flying Corps (Army) and Royal Naval Air Service). Just five days after the L16 and L22 had attacked the region, a meeting at Newcastle was addressed by Mr Pemberton Billing, MP. He called for an imperial air service to be created that would spare expense in building the best machines and enabling Britain to control the skies. He blamed previous political inertia for the current situation and used the example of the L15 which had recently been shot down over London (although attacked by a BE2c aircraft, the L15 was shot down by anti-aircraft fire). *The Times* reported that the overblown accounts of damage made in the German press, was a reaction to the loss of this airship.

Military Hospitals

The severity of the fighting meant that by 1916 it was clear that hospital requirements were quickly being overwhelmed despite several Newcastle civilian hospitals, along with the city's lunatic asylum, and other premises being adapted or converted to serve as military hospitals. The council and the local civilian population were urged to raise funds to make more beds available through the extension of current hospitals and by the building of new ones. The Royal Victoria Infirmary, which during the war was called the 1st Northern General Hospital, had already agreed to be partly converted to a military hospital and placed seven wards, with 200 beds, at the disposal of the government for sick and wounded soldiers. By 1916, the hospital had treated some 5,000 men.[70] The hospital also took over much of nearby Armstrong College for extra ward space.

Due to the demands on medical services brought about by the nature of fighting on the Western Front it became clear that the facilities in Newcastle were becoming stretched to breaking point and improvements were increasingly vital. The 1st Northern General Hospital, subsequently sought public funds in order to expand by adding two new pavilions which provided fifty-two extra beds. Public response was superb and the funds were very quickly raised. Indeed, the first ward was paid for in its entirety by Sir James Knott of Close House. Sir James had lost two of his three sons in the war and the ward was

*Major James
Leadbitter Knott,
DSO, was the third
of all three sons of
Mr James Knott to be
killed whilst serving:
Newcastle Journal,
7 July 1916.*

named in honour of Captain Henry Basil Knott, who was killed aged 24 while serving with the 9th Battalion, Northumberland Fusiliers. Both wards were constructed of wood with felt roofs and built by the hospital staff themselves, were opened in early June and could house sixty-four men. The second ward was also paid for by a single benefactor but in this case the person desired to remain anonymous (tragically Sir James lost a second son just a month after the ward was opened when Major James Leadbitter Knott, DSO, of the 10th Battalion, West Yorkshire Regiment (Prince of Wales's Own) was killed aged 33 on the first day of the Somme – the brothers are buried side-by-side at Ypres Reservoir cemetery). These beds were quickly filled and the hospital campaigned for even more temporary wards to be raised.

The Northumberland No 1 War Hospital was also becoming overstretched and the proposal for a hutted extension was debated by the council and approved pending tenders and inspection of sewer systems by the city engineer. The tenders for the building work were subsequently placed with twelve builders and seven civil engineers. As an indication of the increasing labour shortages due to the wartime situation and the increasing number of government contracts, around half of the building contractors refused to tender due to pressure of work. However, the work, which would provide an extra 540 beds, was quickly undertaken despite an estimated cost of £180,000 (largely because of work needed on new sewer systems) and the hospital gave good service for the rest of the war.

The 1st Northern General Hospital employed a large number of local civilian nursing staff willing and available to take over the duties of the military despite the fact that large numbers of the staff had joined the army or naval nursing services. The nursing staff was aided by volunteer members of the St John's Ambulance Brigade and the British Red Cross, among others. These volunteers worked in the wards alongside the civilian and military staff and were well trained by this point in the war. Many of them subsequently volunteered for overseas service and worked at casualty clearing stations and hospitals in France and Flanders. The buildings of the hospital included specialist wards for electrical treatment, X-ray, inoculations and bacterial investigation. By mid-1916, the hospital had inoculated over 30,000 soldiers prior to their posting abroad. Despite the increasing burden of military cases the hospital still maintained the use of almost 400 beds for civilian patients.[71]

The importance of volunteers and charitable donations remained vital to the work of the military hospitals at Newcastle with appeals being frequently published in the local press. The Ladies Committee of the 1st Northern General Hospital, for example, had weekly appeals in the *Newcastle Daily Journal* asking for gifts of a variety of goods including items such as dry socks, vests, calico and linen, suits, good quality overcoats, chairs, garden seats, also rhubarb and other fresh fruit and vegetables.[72]

Charitable donations towards medical facilities continued unabated throughout the year with funds being raised from private individuals, companies and workers. The enthusiasm of the munitions workers in raising funds contradicted the view held by some of the governing classes and demonstrated a sober commitment to the war effort. The munitions workers of Elswick and Scotswood, for example, raised sufficient money to buy and garage a new motor ambulance, which was built by local company Messrs Angus, Sanderson & Co. on a 20-30hp Armstrong chassis, for the use of the First Aid Nursing Yeomanry Corps at the Front. During the year, munitions workers had also raised funds to supply an X-ray machine to the Northumberland No 1 War Hospital along with over £2,000 to be used to buy various equipment and supplies for the use of wounded soldiers.

A Newcastle steam bus, c.1917-1918. (Newcastle City Library)

Four women employed as drivers by Armstrong-Whitworth's. (Newcastle City Library)

Notes

50   Quoted in Gregory. Adrian: *The Last Great War. British Society and the First World War* (2008), pp. 112-113.

51   Vall. Natasha: *The Emergence of the Post-Industrial Economy in Newcastle 1914-2000*, in Colls, R & Lancaster. B: *Newcastle upon Tyne. A Modern History* (2001), pp. 49-50.

52   Carter. H: *The Control of the Drink Trade: A Contribution to National Efficiency, 1915-17* (1918), pp. 267.

53   Bennison. Brian: 'Drink in Newcastle', in *Newcastle upon Tyne. A Modern History* (2001), pp. 178.

54   Bilton. David: *The Home Front in the Great War* (2003). Kindle edition, Loc. 1874.

55   *Newcastle Daily Journal*, 5 June 1916, pp. 6.

56   *Newcastle Daily Journal*, 7 June 1916, pp. 5.

57   *Newcastle Evening Chronicle*, 1 July 1916, pp. 6.

58   *Newcastle Daily Journal*, 5 July 1916, pp. 10.

59   Supplement to *The London Gazette* (28 July 1917). Available online at [www.london-gazette.co.uk/issues/30209/supplements/7772], accessed 8 November 2013. The action is also described in Sheen, Tyneside Irish, loc. 1676.

60   Sheen, *Tyneside Irish*, loc. 1835.

61   Cooke. Captain C.H. MC: *Historical Records of the 16th (Service) Battalion Northumberland Fusiliers* (1923), pp. 43-46.

62   *The London Gazette*, No. 29740, 8 September 1916.

63   Sheen. John: *Tyneside Scottish. 20th, 21st, 22nd & 23rd (Service) Battalions of the Northumberland Fusilier: A History of the Tyneside Scottish Brigade Raised in the North East in World War One*, (1999) pp. 99.

64   Ibid.

65   Sheen: *Tyneside Irish*, loc. 2095-2104.

66   Sheen: *Tyneside Irish*, loc.2493-2498.

67   *The Times*, 24 January 1916, pp. 10.

68   *Newcastle Evening Chronicle*, 1 August 1916, pp. 5.

69   Coquet & Coast Forum website [http://www.coquetandcoast.co.uk/amble-northumberland/showthread.php?t=168], accessed 12 February 2014.

70   TWAM: HO.RVI/189. Pamphlet: *What the RVI did in the War*, c. 1916, pp. 1-4.

71   TWAM: HO.RVI/189. Pamphlet: *What the RVI did in the War*, c. 1916, pp. 1-4.

72   *Newcastle Daily Journal*, 5 July 1916, pp. 8.

CHAPTER 4

1917
A Peoples' War?

For those employed in the extensive Tyneside shipyards, the year began badly with the news of one of their vessels SS *Ivernia*, a passenger liner converted to troop transport built by Swan Hunter, had been sunk by a submarine in poor weather while carrying troops in the Mediterranean. The losses of ships which men working on the Tyne could remember building was by now growing with every day. The people of Newcastle took a great pride in the ships and the mounting losses due to submarine warfare, which were usually reported in newspapers, could sometimes have a sobering effect on morale.

With the large number of military hospitals and the high rates of military service the sight of wounded soldiers and former soldiers became a common sight to the people of Newcastle with the people organizing days out and parties for wounded servicemen. In recognition of the impact that many of these men's injuries would have on their subsequent lives, a centre for the training of physically disabled former servicemen in non-manual work was opened in the city. The men were trained in a wide variety of professional skills including accountancy, architecture, book-keeping and commercial skills, chemistry, photography and cinematography, also medicine and sanitary inspection.

The military hospitals in Newcastle saw a number of visitors and patients who would go on to acquire some degree of fame. Among these was the composer and poet Ivor Gurney. The Gloucestershire-born Gurney had enlisted in the Gloucestershire Regiment in 1915 as a private and served extensively on the Western Front before being invalided home after being gassed in September 1917. As part of his recovery he was a patient in Newcastle before being posted to recuperate at New Hartley camp. At some point in 1917, one of his fellow patients at New Hartley was the author J.R.R. Tolkien who was being treated for a recurrence of the trench fever which had seen him invalided home in November 1916.

The year brought news of the deaths of men who had connections with Newcastle United; former reserve Richard McGough died of his wounds on 18 April while serving as a bombardier with the 102nd Siege Battery of the Royal Garrison Artillery during the fighting around the village of Feuchy, where he is buried. It is said that former player John Fleming was killed while serving as a major with the East Yorkshire Regiment, but there is no listing of him on the Commonwealth War Graves Commission website or in Officers Died in the Great War.[73]

Food shortages and prices continued to be a source of much comment and concern in Newcastle where, despite increased wages, some families were struggling to purchase staple foodstuffs. Due to the increasing menace of submarine warfare, 500,000t were lost in February alone, combined with Britain's dependence on imported foodstuffs meant that there was a real danger of the country being starved out of the war and that restrictions would have to tighten significantly. To make matters worse the potato harvest was poor and by March there was an acute shortage of the vegetable. In January and February, the newly created Ministry of Food took action to improve the supply situation by ordering millers to drastically increase the amount of flour produced by additional milling or to bulk out the flour by using other cereals. Lord Devonport also issued orders which fixed the price of chocolate and other confectionary which were seen as luxury foods. Other measures included a strong campaign urging for frugality and for the conservation of food while the English and Scottish Co-Operative Wholesale Society purchased 10,000 acres of prime wheat-growing land in Canada. The Saskatchewan-grown wheat would be used to supply the Co-Operative's mills located in five British cities, including Newcastle.

The campaign for frugality and economy of consumption continued throughout the year as the situation became more desperate with local dignitaries keen to play their part in the campaign. In May, the Duke of Northumberland made an impassioned plea in the local press, urging housewives to be more frugal and to limit the consumption of food and especially bread.

The increase in food prices was compounded by the poor potato crop, caused by an outbreak of blight, which led to a potato-shortage and large crowds formed in Newcastle to attempt to purchase the staple vegetable. By early March, shops were finding it increasingly difficult to obtain goods and there was a great rush by customers trying to buy up the last of the supplies. So serious was the situation that many shops were forced to close early and police were often called to disperse angry crowds who had not received their supply. The failure of the potato crop led to a growing demand for potato substitutes and it was a run on these supplies which led to the mayor asking shops to limit customers to their usual amounts and no more. As the blight continued the lack of potatoes quickly became a famine and this caused great hardship for a number of Newcastle families. Extremely long queues built up across the city and there were a number of angry scenes as shops ran out of potatoes and were forced to turn customers away. The Newcastle Co-Operative Society had over 180,000 customers, but was forced to restrict each one to only 2lb of potatoes and even then ran out of supplies leaving hundreds of customers without any which led to angry and potentially violent scenes.

The continuing shortage of potatoes famine led to serious health concerns in Newcastle; there was an outbreak of scurvy which was said to be a direct result of the scarcity and high prices not only of potatoes but of all fresh fruit and vegetables.

The rising number of mercantile shipping casualties and the poor potato crop made the food supply situation in Newcastle worse and became a very serious concern for a majority of residents. The government response to begin the rationing of some foodstuffs led to Newcastle Council appointing an advisory committee to advise the mayor, as he would be responsible for local administration of the scheme.

Delays in the implementation of rationing and price control resulted in further and continued hardship for many of the residents of Newcastle and in June, amid allegations of widespread profiteering, the price of meat began to rise rapidly. On 12 June, the cattle market in the city reported that prices had increased by over 3 shillings in a week and that the price of beef was now at a new high of 23 shillings per stone (14lb).

Another shortage which had a potentially damaging effect on morale was the lack of beer caused by the poor cereal crop and the fact that what was available had been reduced in strength. Most regular drinkers in Newcastle did not approve of the quality of war-time beer but had become accustomed to the self-imposed limited drinking hours. This now became worse as many publicans began shutting an hour earlier (at 8.00pm) because they could not guarantee the supply of beer. A population notoriously keen on drink had already grumblingly accepted the arduous restrictions but this was yet another blow to the morale of the industrial workforce who were increasingly coming to the conclusion that the majority of sacrifice on the home front was being made by themselves and their families.

As shortages and price increases continued unabated the mood of the people began to grow even more suspicious with large numbers believing that the authorities were not interested in fairness and that some traders were in fact determined to profiteer from the situation. Matters came to a head with the appointment of the new Food Committee by the city council. There were immediate and vociferous protests against the constituent make-up of the committee with many Newcastle residents expressing disgust because it was dominated by traders, who they felt had much to be gained by being placed in such a position of power. A letter sent to the council by Lord Rhondda, agreed that a majority of traders on such a committee could be detrimental as it would result in a lack of public confidence. Such was the public hostility towards the committee that they were forced to resign en-masse and a newly-appointed committee was required. Trade union representatives protested that as the main cause of industrial unrest was the unfairness of the price of food they demanded that at least 50 per cent of the new committee should be made up from representatives of the consumer. The council reacted in a manner which did not quite ensure this, but which was somewhat fairer. The mayor decreed that the new committee would consist of six members from the council (two of them representing the Labour Party) and six from outside the council. Aside from the two Labour councillors, the city council representatives consisted of two non-traders and two traders. The outside membership consisted of the manager of the School of Cookery, representatives from the Women's Labour League, the Co-Operative Society, the Butchers' Association, and two non-traders (Sir Thomas Oliver and Mr J.J. Berry). Although this technically meant that 50 per cent were non-traders, several did have close links with trade.

By early October, the government had appointed the regional Food Controller for Newcastle, Northumberland and Durham. This was a former military officer with frontline experience and Major Alexander Leith, MC a colliery owner from Pelaw. Clearly the role did require someone with managerial experience, but in appointing a colliery owner the authorities once again demonstrated a lack of sympathy for the feelings of many working-class families in the region. The appointment came in the shadow of even further price rises. Staples such as bread, sugar, milk and bacon (and of course potatoes) were particularly expensive at this stage of the year with many Newcastle households having to go without these foodstuffs. The higher costs of vegetables and fresh fruit meant that for a large number of residents feeding themselves and their dependents was not only becoming increasingly difficult but that the quality of their diet was deteriorating. For those who were struggling, it was a bitter blow in having to put up with seemingly never ending government campaigns, backed by local dignitaries, urging economy.

Despite the late attempt by government to take some control of the food supply the shortages continued to play an increasingly important role in the lives of many Newcastle families. Despite higher wages for some, the food prices, shortages and increased rate of taxation meant that a significant proportion of residents were finding it increasingly difficult to adequately provide for their families. A number of well attended and vociferous public meetings were held to discuss the matter. The growing anger threatened to spill over into unrest and industrial action; Northumberland miners held a large meeting in the city where they demanded no further decrease in wages until the cost of living was reduced. The people of Newcastle had shown themselves more than willing to make extensive sacrifices for the war effort. But in this third year, there was the worrying sign of the beginning of a sense of war weariness setting in on Tyneside. Although it was true that many Newcastle workers were being paid higher wages they were also facing a vastly increased cost of living (especially in terms of rent and food costs), increased taxation, longer hours, a lack of leisure activities, weariness and worry over friends and family serving abroad. These factors were combining to begin to erode the high morale that had been an almost ever-present factor on Tyneside. The lack of good news on the military front was also beginning to have an effect. The lack of obvious success on the Somme in the previous year along with the huge local casualties suffered was compounded by the overly-optimistic headlines in the press that had accompanied the battle. Now in 1917, it seems that the people of Newcastle had less faith in the military and in what they were being told. The sheer number of ships which were coming into the Tyne for repairs and the daily news of the loss of locally-built ships also resulted in many of the people of Newcastle having a first-hand glimpse of the increasingly grave situation.

However, efforts to bolster morale through visits to the region continued, and in June the King and Queen began an extremely successful two day tour of Tyneside with visits to Newcastle industrial and commercial premises and a special service at the cathedral. During the tour, the royal party visited five shipyards and marine works before touring the city by motorcar to loud cheers from a large, welcoming and enthusiastic crowd. The royal couple also made a journey by motor yacht down the river from Newcastle to the mouth of the Tyne witnessing the full impressive activity of the works on the Tyne. A very favourable impression was made on the King by the efforts of the workers in the yards and by their loyal and enthusiastic commitment to replacing the heavy loss of merchant ships which was having such an impact on the nation. The King also made clear his pleasure with the workers of Newcastle and Tyneside, when the leaders of several trade unions and local MP's were presented to him at a halt in the city.

During the tour of the works the royal guests talked not only to managers but to workers too. The King spoke at length to one 79 year-old shipwright who had worked for many years at the Northumberland Shipbuilding Company. In this yard, the royal couple were also shown work underway on two passenger liners and a large merchant ship along with a demonstration of the armament on a large merchant vessel of the Clan Line. As the King and Queen moved from location to location the streets were lined with workers who had been let out of work to see the couple. At the North Eastern Marine Engineering Works, the King talked at length with a group of workers who had gone back to work after being discharged from military service. He was also impressed by the number of posters around the works which urged economy of consumption.

When the royal couple arrived at Armstrong Whitworth's Walker Yards, they were greeted with a large chalked greeting reading: 'Welcome to canny Walker, there's nee place like Walker'. A large crowd of workers and local residents did their best to reinforce this with loud and prolonged cheering.

The cathedral service was plain and simple with one hymn sung by the choir followed by congregational singing including representatives of the army and navy along with the mayor, members of the council, Armstrong College and other local institutions also a number of invited Newcastle residents.

After the service, the royal party made its way to St James' Park where an investiture was to take place. This was to present more than 100 local soldiers with awards for valour. Also present, was a large group of black-clothed men and women who were in mourning for a family member lost on active service. The ceremony was watched by an estimated 50,000 spectators who greeted the arrival of then King with loud and prolonged cheers. After Brigadier-General English had been awarded the Cross of St Michael and St George and the DSO to two officers, the crowd erupted into thunderous applause when the Victoria Cross was awarded to Lance Corporal Thomas Bryan of the Northumberland Fusiliers (Bryan received the medal for eliminating an enemy machine-gun position). Many other men followed to be awarded the Distinguished Conduct Medal or the Military Medal and each was loudly cheered by the enthusiastic crowd, particularly those who were from the Northumberland Fusiliers or the Durham Light Infantry or those who had wound stripes on their arms.

The ceremony concluded with a much sadder event as the mourners were called forward one-by-one to be presented to the royal couple. They were led by the widow and son of Captain Roy Dunford who had been killed in action and the King and Queen together presented Mrs Dunford with her husband's DSO and talked to both widow and child. The cheers at this point were more muted and a hushed and respectful atmosphere prevailed. For several of the widows the event proved too emotional and one collapsed after being awarded her late husband's Military Medal, and had to be assisted by the crowd. Two other women departed the dais in tears and many of the crowd reacted emotionally.

Further cheers occurred when awards were made to a father in khaki who was accepting his son's medal posthumously. The investiture was concluded by three rousing cheers for the King and three more for the Queen.

After the visit, the King conveyed his thanks to the people of the North-East and stated that their, 'outspoken sympathy [filled] him with courage and confidence'. He went on to say that the loyalty, fortitude and devotion of the workers of the area assured him that the industrial army of the north was strong and would provide the means for victory.

Newcastle remained committed to the war effort and, despite brief drops in morale, was even enthusiastically supportive. This was reflected in the popularity of a demonstration held on the Town Moor in July, which was protesting against the small amount of pacifist propaganda which had appeared recently in some of the Newcastle munitions works.

Female footballers from Elswick. (Illustrated Chronicle)

The increasing importance of the contribution made by women in Newcastle was becoming more apparent as it became an ever more common site to see large numbers of female munitions workers, clerical staff, bus conductors and other workers going to and from work. The general public had by now accepted that women were taking these roles and most appreciated they were proving themselves every bit as capable as the men they replaced. The growing importance of women in the military was also becoming marked as the Newcastle public, well used to seeing civilian volunteer nursing staff, became more aware of seeing women in military uniform. Local newspapers advertised for women to work as drivers with the various armed forces and, due to its growing importance, particularly in early 1917 advertisements for women to serve as drivers in the Royal Flying Corps. Local companies were again quick to take advantage of the opportunities offered by these events and advertisements appeared in local newspapers by companies such as The Northern Counties Motor School, registered training providers for the services.

The demands for and, increasingly, the importance of women in vital war work was highlighted in September by a government appeal for a further

10,000 to join the Women's Army Auxiliary Corps for service at home or abroad. In order to recruit the women, regional offices were set up under the command of a regional controller with Newcastle, as one of the major sources of volunteers, selected as the location of one of the offices.

Events abroad also continued to be of interest to the general public and the overthrow of the Tsar and subsequent change of government in Russia was a popular talking point. Such was the impact of the event on the people of Newcastle, and motivated partially, one suspects, by the importance of Russian naval contracts with Tyneside companies, that the mayor sent a letter congratulating the Russian people and the Duma on the establishment of democratic government and hoping that this would see a successful prosecution of the war.

A common theme throughout Newcastle's wartime experience was the importance of the continuation of some sporting events in order to provide leisure, interest and a sense of normality. The Easter holiday was a particularly popular time for such events with golf tournaments, women's football and other sports. In 1917, a large pedestrianism (a popular pre-war Tyneside sport) contest was held at the Victoria Grounds. The importance placed on this meeting can be seen by the fact that not inconsiderable

Blyth Spartans female football team after winning the cup at St James'.
(Illustrated Chronicle)

Womens' teams sometimes played against their male equivalents who were 'handicapped' (in this case with arms tied behind their backs). (Illustrated Chronicle)

prizes of £100, £40 and £25 were to be awarded for the three main races. The draw was to take place at the Farmer's Inn, Scotswood Road, and the races would take place over two days with the main event being a 220yd handicap race which attracted 172 entries. The majority of competitors were from Newcastle and nearby towns, but several had travelled from farther afield including Sunderland, Edinburgh, Sheffield, Glasgow, Carlisle and even Cork in Ireland. Other events included a 60yd handicap, a 50yd handicap for veterans and a 130yd race which attracted a further 130 competitors.

The enthusiasm for the war effort continued to be generally high. This was proven by the response to the National Service Week in March, which saw almost every house in the city visited and a large number of volunteers recruited.

Despite ongoing, everyday minor misdemeanours, serious criminal activity had dropped in the city to such an extent that the most recent sitting of the sessions had, for the first time, dispensed with the need for a grand jury as there were no cases of sufficient severity to warrant the need. Throughout the year, the most frequent crime remained petty theft which could largely be linked to poverty and to the failure of wages to keep pace with the vastly increased cost of living. Theft of foodstuffs and clothing were relatively commonplace although usually very small in nature. There remained those who were willing to take advantage of their position in order to make a profit from the wartime situation. In July, Sergeant George Ronaldson of Newcastle City Police was sentenced to eighteen months imprisonment for breaking into the Co-Operative Stores and stealing pairs of boots.

Despite the generally positive morale on Tyneside there were those who sought to continue with criminal activities. These were avidly reported in the local press as both a warning and an encouragement to the people of Newcastle. Many of the incidents were relatively trivial and the vast majority had little or no impact on or linked to wartime conditions. Many of the cases seem to have involved young men who for one reason or another had not been called up. A typical example occurred in early 1917, when 18 year-old John Livingstone Holland was prosecuted for larceny and embezzlement. Holland was accused of having stolen a watch, an overcoat, a jacket and other items from Tower House and when arrested was wearing some of the stolen items. He was further accused of having stolen from his employer Thomas Harper, a coal merchant, of Falconer Street. When sent to deliver a ton of coal valued at 26 shilling he had spent the money collected. The young man had been previously employed at the Walker Yard, but had chosen to run away from his job without obtaining a leaving certificate (an offence during the war). It seems clear that Holland came from a somewhat disrupted home as his father appeared to further implicate his son by saying that he could earn as much as 30 shillings and 6 pence per week and was in lodging rooms. In mitigation, Holland claimed that he had left home because every time he went there he was 'played war with' and that he had 'chucked' his job at the Walker Yard. Holland had little choice but to plead guilty to both charges.[74]

The crime which seemed to inflame the most impassioned response in Newcastle was that of profiteering. Obviously the entire population was suffering hardships but these were easier to bear if one could believe that everybody was making an equal sacrifice. Thus, to see a shopkeeper or businessman making large profits from the war while at the same time appearing to drive prices up and contribute little to the war effort, greatly angered the average man or woman. Such cases always received press attention and aroused bitter and acrimonious comment. One such case was that of Mr John Robert Jull and Thomas Hunt, the manager and assistant manager, of St Anthony's Co-Operative Society who were charged in April

Newcastle Corporation's electric tramcars continued to provide good service throughout the war. They also continued to advertise popular wartime products such as Andrews' Liver Salts. The photo is from Byker Depot in 1917. (Newcastle City Library)

with attempting to supply sugar with additional conditions. The accused had demanded that a customer, who happened to be a soldier's wife with five children, first spend 2 shillings on other goods before they would agree to sell her sugar. Obviously, this was seen as a blatant case of profiteering and a harsh view was taken. The chairman was in particular scathing in his remarks when he commented that the, 'sugar supply had been scandalous and [he had] only been lenient as this was the first offence [he had seen] under the new Food Controllers Order'. Mr Jull was fined the sum of £5 and his co-accused the sum of £1.[75]

Drunkenness and the new laws laid down to prevent this along with the early closing of bars and clubs also resulted in a number of, sometimes overzealous, prosecutions in Newcastle with the National Union of Gas Worker's & General Labourers Club in Scotswood Road being prosecuted. The steward and chairman were both charged with supplying intoxicating liquor after hours in April. A subsequent investigation of the clubs' accounts showed that with a membership fee of 1 shilling plus a further contribution of 1 shilling per week the club had taken £84 since January and that £105 16 shillings and 8 pence had been spent on liquor of which only 7 shillings and 6 pence had been spent on mineral water and 13 shillings on cigarettes. Clearly this was a hard drinking club membership and the figures clearly demonstrate the popularity of working men's clubs in the city during the period. The fine imposed was strict, both the steward and chairman were fined £3, an order for striking

Conductress at Newcastle worked on both the trams and omnibuses: Daily Mirror, 20 May 1915.

the club off the register was to be sought and the premises was banned from operating as a club for a year. Clearly the authorities were still very keen to crack down on what they saw as a culture of the over-indulgence of drink among industrial workers in Newcastle and this explains the often harsh penalties which were imposed for sometimes relatively minor offences. Throughout the year the laws concerning the consumption of alcohol continued to be strenuously enforced. In early September, two men fined the large sum of £50 each for the crime of drinking during prohibited hours.

As throughout the war the majority of crimes in Newcastle were of the type that took place regardless of the national situation, but others were as a result of the influx of newcomers to the city. In December, for example, William Cavanagh a 29 year-old from Newcastle became the only man to be executed in the city during the war after being convicted of the stabbing to death of Henry Arthur Hollyer, a 27 year-old naval seaman from London, at 1 West Street, Newcastle in June.

Although the authorities fretted about drunkenness and absenteeism along with the collapse of moral rectitude, as seen by an increase in the number of prosecutions for prostitution and the increase of venereal disease cases (particularly amongst the army), members of the general public reserved their outrage for crimes involving corruption such as profiteering or frauds which involved dodging service. One such scandal erupted around the Royal Marine Submarine Miners, with headquarters was in Newcastle, when it was alleged that a captain had been arranging for men to join the unit in return for bribes. Captain John Morales was said to have arranged with a number of local men to show preference in their recruitment to the unit in exchange for considerable sums of money. It was believed that the men wished to serve their country without the chance of foreign-service so that they could carry on their business interests while serving their country in a relatively low-risk service. Newcastle City Police had heard rumours of this and used an undercover agent who, posing as a businessman was offered a place in the unit for the sum of £100. After his acceptance of the payment, Captain Morales was arrested and appeared before magistrates who placed him on remanded. The deputy town clerk, Mr Bateson, claimed at the hearing that the case was a very serious one with wide ramifications and that further arrests were pending.[76] The very next day, one Private Hyman Cohen, a moneylender, was arrested in Doncaster and charged at Newcastle with acting as go-between between potential recruits and Captain Morales. Another undercover officer had been told by Mr Cohen that the sum to join the unit was in the region of £250.[77]

Further arrests were made, including one Private Herbert Pearson (a pawnbroker from Spennymoor). At the end of July, the commanding officer Colonel F.G. Scott, and two privates, William Hood Bowman (a Westoe estate agent) and David Walter Kirkup (a dentist from South Shields), were also charged. The colonel was charged with accepting money for showing favouritism in recruitment and there were claims that the police had direct evidence showing that the colonel had accepted payments. Private Bowman was alleged to have paid £200 for entry and Kirkup had been told that unless he paid £45 he would be transferred to Orkney or the Shetlands. All three defendants were remanded into custody.[78] On Thursday, 26 July, the six men appeared in court, and Colonel Scott and Captain Morales were remanded again and the privates were released on bail of £500 and with sureties of £250.[79]

At court, further charges were brought and evidence given by a number of witnesses including bank clerks who gave details of the payments. It also emerged that Captain Morales had money paid to him by a police agent in his possession when arrested. On the second day, Private Hyman Cohen gave evidence that he had been attested under the Derby Scheme in 1916, but had been approached by Captain Morales because he had a motorcar and the unit required a member with a vehicle for the use by the commanding officer. After he had joined the unit Cohen had applied for a commission, but was told by Morales that a vacancy would have to be created by paying a current member to leave and also that Morales would 'want a bit' for himself. The prosecutor dropped the charges against two of the defendants who were testifying against others with Pearson claiming that he paid Morales £400 of the £425 requested to join the unit.[80]

On Friday, 24 August, the man who had acted as a police agent gave his evidence. Mr Robert Purdie Mitchell Wilson, a dental mechanic, stated that he had a conversation with Hyman Cohen in late June about his business and the fact that he had recently been called up for the army. Wilson alleged that Cohen told him that if he could be classified as lower than general service he might be able to help him. A further meeting saw Cohen tell Wilson that it would cost him £250 and that Cohen did not keep the money but he was allowed leave to carry on his business. Cohen wrote a letter of introduction to Colonel Scott and gave it to Wilson. The witness showed the letter to the police who returned it and told him to carry on with the scheme under their supervision. A meeting with Captain Morales was arranged and Wilson was told that the total cost to join would be £400. The police supplied a down-payment of £100 which the witness handed over to Morales. After accepting the payment Morales was arrested.[81]

On 28 August, there were further charges preferred against Colonel Scott under the Prevention of Corruption Act. In addition, Scott was now charged with having accepted a £200 bribe to admit Jacob Cohen to his unit and with accepting two cases of brandy to keep Baron Abrahams in a certain posting. Abrahams, an auctioneer, gave evidence claiming that after being rated as B1 by the Derby Scheme he had been considering which unit to join when he was told that for £150 (divided between Morales and Scott) he would be enlisted by the Royal Marine Submarine Miners. Abrahams paid the sum and was told by Morales, 'It's no use beating about the bush; the £150 has passed you. You are a lucky fellow getting into the corps, because you are the last recruit who will be able to get in.' A further £25 was requested if he wished to serve in the headquarters and when it seemed likely he would be posted to Scotland he had Scott cancel the posting on the condition that Abrahams purchase a gift for the commanding officer; he subsequently paid £11 2 shillings for two cases of brandy and had them sent to the colonel. However, under cross-examination an orderly remembered taking delivery of the brandy at Scott's home and claimed he placed it under a table but had not told Scott. A police superintendent then gave evidence that during a search of Scott's house promissory notes to the sum of £13,635 were found indicating that Scott had been acting as an unlicensed moneylender.[82] At the conclusion of prosecution evidence Colonel Scott and Captain Morales pleaded not guilty to all charges while Cohen pleaded guilty to conspiracy, but not guilty to the other charges.[83]

Over the course of several days in November the case was heard at Newcastle Assizes by Mr Justice Salter. Cohen and Morales both pleaded guilty to the charged preferred against them while Colonel Scott pleaded not guilty to all charges. After hearing the evidence the jury arrived at a guilty verdict on Scott and Mr Justice Salter sentenced him to eighteen months imprisonment while Morales was sentenced to fifteen months and Cohen to eight months. All three were also ordered to pay the sum of £200 each towards the cost of the trial. In summing up, Mr Justice Salter emphasized the seriousness of the case and stated that it was hard for him to believe that such a scheme of corruption could have taken place without the knowledge and collusion of Colonel Scott as commanding officer.[84] As a direct result of this case the headquarters of the units was moved from Newcastle to the south coast.

Nationally, the growing war weariness and increasing industrial tension did see an upturn in pacifist campaigning, but this was not welcomed on Tyneside with the vast majority being opposed, sometimes violently so, to pacifist meetings and campaigns. An attempt to set up a conference supporting the Workers' and Soldiers' Council resulted in violent scenes of disorder. The group had initially wanted to hold the conference in the town hall but the council refused permission and the venue was changed to a smaller building. A large and vocal crowd had gathered outside to protest against the meeting and as the platform party prepared to take their seats fights broke out and some of the crowd forced their way inside. A large number of protesters were in uniform or were former soldiers and several stormed the stage with one man in a civilian coat with a wound stripe bared his arm showing a war wound and demonstrated his anger by shouting: 'That is what I have got for fighting for traitors'. The situation became worse when a group of colonials invaded the stage during the fist fights and the meeting was completely broken up before being abandoned.[85]

With the large numbers of soldiers and families with members in the forces along with huge numbers employed in the munitions industries, it was extremely unlikely that pacifist groups would be able to establish themselves in Newcastle. Throughout the war, the residents of the city were widely supportive of the war effort and a substantial number were violently opposed to any pacifistic group or proposal. Indeed, the workers were quite capable of reacting against what they saw as a lack of determination in their leaders. This was shown demonstrated by the numbers of Northumberland miners' lodges which censured their leadership for attending pacifist conferences.

As some people prematurely turned their thoughts towards peace and matters such as post-war trade issues, the people of Newcastle received a wake-up call when a naval action took place on their 'doorstep' just off the mouth of the Tyne. German destroyers managed to penetrate British naval defences and attacked two trawlers, sinking one, also two neutral vessels, both of which were sunk. Later on the same day, a convoy heading for Norway from Scotland was attacked by four German destroyers (possibly the same ships). The convoy was supposed to have a fleet escort but this had not arrived and instead the merchant ships were escorted by two light ant-submarine destroyers and four armed trawlers. Completely outmatched the British destroyer HMS *Partridge* (launched at Swan Hunter in 1916) was quickly sunk and her sister-ship HMS *Pellew* was crippled and forced to withdraw. The four trawlers were quickly destroyed and all the merchant ships sunk; that the enemy could raid, seemingly at will, at this stage of the war was seen as a shameful disgrace by the people of Newcastle and caused some alarm and consternation expressed by letters in the local press.

The year had been a bleak one; civilian suffering in Newcastle caused by shortages and price rises being matched by the bleak news from the Front. The huge offensives of 1917 with large battles at Arras, Vimy Ridge, the Scarpe, the Hindenburg Line, Messines and Ypres had all resulted in costly stalemates. For the people of Newcastle, they resulted in further heavy casualties in men from the city and for bereaved families even greater struggles to come. While the church and others talked of victory for the ordinary folk of Newcastle the war was an uncertain grinding process which was leaving large parts of the population increasingly war-weary.

There was a growing dislocation in Newcastle society between the establishment and the ordinary people of the city. The establishment seemed to be determined to press on and to pay little heed to the everyday hardships being suffered by the ordinary people and remained determined to inculcate a sense of moral superiority and cocksure belief in victory. Nowhere was this demonstrated more clearly than in the churches. To commemorate the third anniversary of the beginning of the war, church services were held across the city with the clergy by and large anxious to continue to rally support for the aims of the war and to accentuate the positives of Britain's moral stance. The Bishop of Newcastle summed this up in a piece he wrote for the diocesan magazine in which he stated, that while the mood of the congregation was sombre and lacked boastfulness there was a continued determination to right the morale wrongs, such as the ravaging of Belgium, that had been perpetrated and to ensure that, by winning the war, these wrongs could not be repeated. Yet a study of letters to the local press reveals little interest in the struggles of Belgium, but instead a focus on the shortages, high prices and perceived corruption that was belittling the sacrifices being made by the services.

As 1917 ended there seemed, to the majority, to be no end in sight to the war and victory was increasingly in doubt. The people of Newcastle were increasingly becoming weary of the constant strain and the impact of food shortages and increases in the cost of living. December 1917 was bleak, and it seemed that the weather was determined to reflect the mood when gales and snowstorms battered the city for over twenty-four hours over the Christmas period. On Boxing Day over 3in of snow fell. In Newcastle the population wearily, though loyally, ruminated on a fifth year of war, anxiety, shortages and uncertainty.

Industry

Enquiries into the reasons for absenteeism among munitions workers and particularly shipyard workers continued throughout the year with strenuous and, at times, vitriolic arguments put forward by all sides. The evidence seems to clearly show that, contradictory to the arguments put forward by many employers, drunkenness was not a major factor. Indeed, on 2 January, despite the shipyards being on holiday, there were very few cases of drunkenness put before Newcastle magistrates. This was in no doubt partly due to the harsh licensing restrictions already in operation which ensured that obtaining drink at particular times was very difficult. Those who had made extensive studied of rates of absenteeism came to the conclusion that the main factor was the differences in scales of pay for different trades. Boilermakers, riveters, caulkers and platers in Newcastle were finding that they could earn high wages by working for only three to four days a week. This, combined with anger over the rates of income tax, resulted in men deciding that there was little point in working hours beyond what was needed to support their families, if it was to simply be taken from them in punitive taxes. It was argued that even the total prohibition of alcohol would not alter this as the men were unwilling to risk their health working unnecessary hours only for their reward to be taken from them by the government. A further point of contention was the unwillingness of the government to provide a tax break for workers who sometimes had to supply some of their own tools and to travel for work. The other important reason for absenteeism was the nature of the job. The main work undertaken in the shipyards was heavy and exhausting. It was found that, given the increase in hours and the pace of work demanded, men were struggling to work for week after week with few or no breaks.

Although the vast majority of Newcastle munitions workers were committed and did a fantastic job in very trying circumstances, it is likely that there was a significant minority who were willing to absent themselves from work for frivolous reasons such as drinking, gambling or attending sporting events. The authorities in the city dealt harshly with those who were found to be repeat offenders and there were cases where men were warned and then fined before being threatened with imprisonment or enforced enlistment in the army. The unions were aware of some malingerers, but argued that the procedural process of bringing men before an industrial tribunal, at which these men were dealt with, simply resulted in more lost time and increased resentment in the workforce. They argued that it would be better to refer such matters to the unions and to let them deal with the disciplinary hearings through fines and suspension of union benefits.

The employers were increasingly unhappy with the procedure of bringing cases before a tribunal as they were seeing relations with their workforce suffer as a result, Also every case necessitated the loss of at least one member of staff to present the case to the tribunal and subsequently even more lost time. The employers argued that as the scheme was imposed upon them by the government then it would be fairer for the Ministry of Munitions to prosecute the cases.

A leafy Osborne Road, Jesmond with a tram and parked motor. Visiting Russian engineer, Yevgeni Zamyatin, was disgusted by the gentlemen of the suburb during his wartime stay. (Newcastle City Library)

The losses being suffered by the merchant fleet due to unrestricted submarine warfare continued to mount and the initial reluctance of the Admiralty to institute a convoy system resulted in a great deal of work for the local shipyards and repair yards. However, despite being exceptionally busy with essential war work Armstrong Whitworth also found time to fulfil contracts for allied governments such as Russia. Many of the contracts were for icebreakers and two vessels, the *Sviatogor* and the *Saint Alexander Nevski*, were completed in 1917. The vessels were built under the supervision of a Russian delegate named Yevgeny Zamyatin, who was an engineer and writer resided in Jesmond for two years. He was not impressed with what he found and saw the people of Jesmond as being hopelessly bourgeois and unimaginative. He seemed to be particularly irritated by the habit of gentlemen to dress similarly (presumably in their best suits) on Sundays.[86]

While the shipyards were booming and producing new vessels at a prodigious rate the ship owners in Newcastle were still concerned over what they viewed as the waste that was being caused by government control (by this point 80 per cent of Newcastle owned vessels had been commandeered by the government) and by the inefficient use of ships by the Admiralty and the army. Sir Walter Runciman addressed these concerns at the annual meeting of the Moor Line in Newcastle and went on to state that ships were being turned around too slowly due to a lack of dock-side labour also that losses of merchant ships were not being replaced quickly enough due to a lack of skilled labour in the shipyards and by an over-commitment on the part of the government to naval-building programmes over mercantile contracts.

Manpower demands continued to cause some problems in the city with some companies finding it difficult to secure enough skilled labour and finding that the numbers of those who had been brought in to dilute the labour pool (mainly women and the unskilled) were beginning to run low. The government responded to this national problem by creating a new government department and looking at new ways to control the labour market. As a result of this the scheme of universal national service put forward by Neville Chamberlain. The scheme was designed primarily to ensure that men and women could be directed into vital industries in order to solve manpower shortages and the impact of absenteeism and also the lack of skilled labour. The creation of the new Department of National Service resulted in further promotion for a former Lord Mayor of Newcastle. Colonel Johnstone Wallace, who sat as chairman of the Newcastle Military Tribunal and the local committee of the Ministry of Munitions, for the training of workers and dilution of labour, was selected to fill the role of deputy director of the Trades Section of National Service.

However, as the war dragged on and the cost of living rose steadily, an increasing number of Newcastle workers began to feel that they were being exploited by the government and the common good feeling that had predominated in the city began to show the first signs of crumbling. Resentment amongst workers was now at a greater level than at any other time since the war began and was compounded by rises in the cost of living and food shortages (it was estimated that the cost of living was increasing by 27 per cent per year). In March, engineers on the Tyne came out on an illegal strike for better working conditions (particularly a shorter working day) and better pay but mainly over the question of dilution of labour allowing un-skilled workers to operate machinery. The Minister of Labour reacted promptly by issuing a statement declaring his concern over the loss of munitions production and the dangers that this posed to the war effort and offered to organize a hearing into the causes of the strike within a week if the men returned to work at once. The machine workers did indeed decide to return to work the next day and it was felt that the members of the Amalgamated Society of Engineers (ASE) would also decide to return, as long as the minister was true to his promise of an early hearing. The ASE and the strike had gained little popular support on Tyneside, as there was a view that the engineers were among those trades which were willing to make a profit from the war while being unwilling to provide volunteers for service abroad. The Committee of Production met days afterwards to discuss the matter and made an offer of an increase of 2 shillings per week on time rates and an increase in piece rates. The strike was thus quickly resolved and short lived.

Efforts to assure the Newcastle shipyard workers that their contribution was particularly valued continued with further tours by VIP's. In April, this included the Prime Minister of New Zealand who toured the shipyards and linked the production of merchant vessels to the food crisis by drawing attention to the 3,500,000 animal carcasses being held in cold storage in New Zealand due to the lack of available shipping. Clearly such speeches were intended not only to reassure the workers and to boost morale, but also to encourage even greater productivity by offering a better future to the workers. In Newcastle, many people at this time were suffering from the rising food prices and from a general rise in the cost of living. However, most were not gullible enough to merely accept such basic arguments and many were increasingly willing to instead blame the government for not ensuring adequate supplies of food or controlling price rises.

However, it has to be said that Newcastle generally continued to have a good reputation as far as labour matters were concerned and the area including the city witnessed far fewer strikes than in comparable areas of the country. Indeed, such was the lack of industrial unrest that Mr John Barker, the head of the local Boilermakers' Society, could proudly claim that the society had paid out less than £250 in strike pay in the previous three years.

Indeed, the workers of the city continued to back the war effort to an extraordinary degree. As the focal centre of a vast industrial area Newcastle was often the scene of meetings by a variety of industrial organizations. For example, a conference of over 250 different industrial organizations and friendly societies representing some 200,000 people from Newcastle, Northumberland, Durham, Cumberland and Cleveland met in the city in mid-July to organize a citizens' and service committee in order to counteract the propaganda which was being spread by the pacifist groups that had been present at the Leeds Convention (largely the United Socialist Council). The convention was also vehemently opposed to the opinions of Ramsay MacDonald and pledged its allegiance to the government in its prosecution of the war. At its conclusion the conference also passed a motion calling for preparation for demobilisation and industry at the successful conclusion of the war.

Notes

73 Fleming is noted as a casualty on the forum section of The Long, Long Trail website [www.1914-1918. invisionzone.com/forums/index.php?showtopic=15320], accessed 20 December 2013.

74 *Newcastle Evening Chronicle*, 2 April 1917, pp. 6.

75 *Newcastle Evening Chronicle*, 3 April 1917, pp. 4.

76 *The Times*, 11 July 1917, pp. 8.

77 Ibid, 13 July 1917, pp. 3.

78 *The Times*, 24 July 1917, pp. 3.

79 *The Times*, 27 July 1917, pp. 3.

80 *The Times*, 15 August 1917, pp. 3.

81 Ibid, 25 August 1917, pp. 3.

82 Ibid, 29 August 1917, pp. 8.

83 Ibid, 21 September 1917, pp. 3.

84 Ibid, 12 November 1917, pp. 4.

85 *The Times*, 30 July 1917, pp. 3.

86 Moffat, Alistair & Rosie, George: *Tyneside: A History of Newcastle and Gateshead from Earliest Times* (2006), pp. 309.

CHAPTER 5

1918
Disaster into Victory, and Peace

Industry

The contribution to the war effort by Armstrong Whitworth had been unprecedented. By the end of the war, the company had manufactured forty-seven warships, 230 armed-merchant vessels, 102 tanks, over 100 of their own aircraft, many other aircraft built under license, several airships, 13,000 artillery pieces, 12,000 gun carriages, 14,500,000 shells, 18,500,000 million fuses and 21,000,000 cartridge cases.[87] To accurately reflect the scale of this it must be remembered that by the end of the war the British Expeditionary Force (BEF) required 6,437 artillery pieces; Armstrong Whitworth had, over the course of the war, produced 201 per cent of this total. Even in terms of aircraft which was always a fairly minor sideline for the company they had, over the course of the war, produced over 10 per cent of the total number of aircraft in service with the RFC in France. Many of the later aircraft were the FK 8 reconnaissance/bomber which, although eclipsed in number by the Royal Aircraft Establishment RE8, was widely appreciated by crews for its durability and the fact that the type had dual controls allowing an observer a chance of returning if his pilot was injured. The FK 8 was more popular than its more prominent competitor and served with five squadrons on the Western Front, with three home defence squadrons, two partial squadrons in Macedonia, one in Palestine and at least nine training squadrons.

The number of employees at Armstrong Whitworth had increased by almost 300 per cent to almost 60,000. The company which had gone through its golden period under the entrepreneurial and scientific genius

A heavy railway howitzer manufactured by Armstrong's.

Siege artillery 'Hilda'. Typical of pieces manufactured at Elswick.

and stewardship of its founder in the Victorian era had been buoyed by the war and had undergone a wartime boom. There were, however, negatives which explain the relatively poor post-war performance. Foremost of these was an over-dependence on government work and a narrow focus on munitions and shipbuilding which, while ideally suited to most of the Victorian era and all of the war, was less suited to peacetime productivity and profitability. The company also seemed to suffer, along with other Tyneside businesses, from a lack of entrepreneurial ingenuity and a subsequent failure to expand into and exploit new markets. The case of the company's attitude towards production of motor vehicles demonstrates this clearly. In 1912, Armstrong Whitworth produced 344 motorcars, but this compared very poorly with the 1,000 Ford Model T motorcars produced every day! Although the company did see the possibilities, the concentration of munitions production on Tyneside had led to the plant becoming specialized and opportunities for updating were missed. In 1919, motor vehicle production was merged with Siddeley-Deasy at Coventry[88] and all vehicles produced from then on were sold as Armstrong-Siddeley.

Anti-aircraft gun made at Armstrong's.

Armstrong Whitworth FK8.

Armstrong Whitworth quadruplane.

Other large manufacturers made impressive contributions; the Low Walker Yard of Swan Hunter & Wigham Richardson operated as a factory where female workers produced high-explosive shells for the military. At the end of the war the women were thanked, treated to a lunch and given presents of jewellery before being dismissed to make way for men to take their places.[89] The Parsons workshops, in addition to their marine engineering work, also manufactured reflectors for military searchlights which were used on both the Western and Home Fronts.

Although the First World War has been described as a watershed moment for women in the workplace this can be queried in Newcastle. Certainly the workers' settlement which saw them acquiesce to the dilution of labour restricted the numbers of women employed in heavy engineering. In Newcastle, the numbers remained consistently below the national average with, for example, only 7 per cent (150 women) of the workforce employed at the St Peter's Basin Engine Works site of Hawthorn Leslie were women as compared to the national average of 31 per cent.[90] Despite this, there were a large number of women working in industry in Newcastle by the end of the war with large numbers also working in the offices taking the place of

One of the motor cars produced by Armstrong-Whitworth's. (Newcastle City Library)

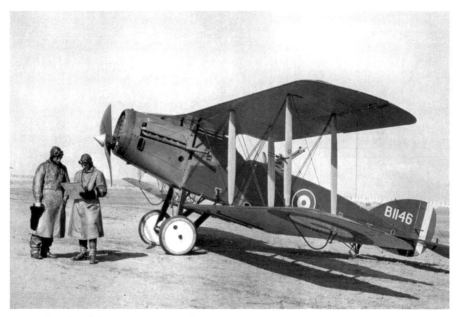

Bristol F2b of the type built under license in Newcastle.

male clerks. Many others worked in diverse areas, including public transport and agriculture.

Throughout the war the industries in Newcastle and Tyneside had benefited from an abundance of government orders and the shipbuilding industry had also benefited from orders to replace merchant ships lost to the enemy. Other industries were able to increase their orders as a result of this improvement in the financial situation. The area was also able to benefit from a fairly peaceful industrial relations situation throughout the war. Newcastle and Tyneside did not see major strikes and the workers seem to have been generally, and genuinely, patriotic in their approach to industrial relations. This could perhaps be partially explained by the high-recruitment rates in the city as many workers would have had relatives, friends or colleagues who were serving abroad and this could have spurred them on to patriotic efforts. The lack of an organized workers committee on Tyneside, and the opposition to the creation of such a body, also resulted in a more passive workforce with James Hinton claiming that the lack of a committee meaning that, 'Tyneside was the most important gap in the development of the shop stewards' movement'.[91] Once again this demonstrates the innate conservatism of the Tyneside working class of the time. Other factors producing relative harmony in industrial relations during

A group of female munitions workers from Armstrong-Whitworth's. (Newcastle City Library)

the war included the higher wages that were obtainable for the majority of those involved in the munitions industries.

Because of its industrial nature, Newcastle continued to witness more than its fair share of industrial intrigue and, despite the lack of disputes within the city it played host to a number of meetings which resulted from national disputes. In January, for example, the ASE was again in dispute, but this time primarily with other unions. As the previous years' dispute had made clear, the support for the ASE was very weak amongst other unions and many viewed the engineers with apathy and thinly disguised hostility. The dispute centred on the agreement which meant that the ASE would be consulted separately from other unions if the government wished to alter the schedule of protected occupations. Other unions were in favour of joint consultation. The clear solution was for a joint conference, the ASE was insisting on a separate meeting with the government but the government was unable to accept as this would cause conflict with the other unions. A large meeting of the ASE was held in Newcastle in early February at which the members voted to support their committee. Some delegates attempted to 'highjack' the meeting by introducing pacifist amendments but it was reported that these received short shrift from the assembled members.

Although the government continued to drive the munitions industries to exhaustion, it also removed some of the available workforce as the shortage of men in the army became critical when the German Army, reinforced by the freeing up of men after Russia's withdrawal from the war, launched a massive offensive at the end of March which quickly broke the Allied lines and threatened Paris. Clearly the offensive, if successful, could end the war before the US Army was able to fully mobilize. The seriousness of the situation was reported to the people of Newcastle in daily newspaper accounts and in reaction the population were alternatively angered and anxious. For some Newcastle munitions workers it also meant the loss of their relatively well-paid jobs as Lloyd George ordered a review of munitions workers (along with miners, transport workers and civil servants) in order to force more men into the army; the age of military service was also raised to 50 years-old.

The seriousness of the situation in France was reflected on Tyneside and the people of Newcastle once again demonstrated their commitment to the nation's war effort. For some time there had been a growing mood of agitation and dissatisfaction amongst munitions workers. On 21 July, the Ministry of Munitions even took the dramatic step of urging munitions workers not to

Munitions girls in fancy dress for Newcastle's Rose Day Festival which celebrated the contribution of the women to the war effort and raised funds for the troops: Daily Mirror, 13 August 1918.

More munitions girls during Rose Day. Central to the festival was the seven mile procession of the women, many of whom had just finished a shift: Daily Mirror, 13 August 1918.

strike during the critical battle. In other parts of the country, the appeal was unsuccessful with munitions workers striking in Coventry and Birmingham just days later. The strike was only ended when the government threatened the strikers by declaring that if they did not return to work they would be conscripted. However, in Newcastle there was little disruption and the vast majority of workers continued as normal.

Although many Newcastle men were conscripted following these moves the government was keenly aware of how vital Tyneside industry was to the war effort and even while attempting to recruit men from less skilled roles for the army it evolved a strategy of releasing men currently serving who had valuable skills in munitions work, and particularly shipbuilding. The growing losses of merchant ships were reaching crisis levels and, despite herculean efforts, the shipyards and repairers were now struggling to cope with the required levels of work. Labour shortages, especially those of skilled workers, were biting and the dilution of labour could only accomplish so much as newcomers into the yards still required to be trained. As a result of this, a government order to home-based army units to release qualified shipyard workers so that they could return to increasingly vital work. A large number of Newcastle shipyard workers had joined up but the majority were serving abroad. Others, many of who had been wounded and when considered fit for limited duty, not service abroad, but serving in home defence units were now to be released for work in their previous occupations where possible. A schedule of release, organized by age and occupation, was published which ordered the release of men from age 19 (for platers, shipwrights, caulkers, etc.) to men 32 years-old (fitters, turners, machine operators, erectors and pattern makers).

The government also reorganized the processes of organizing the shipyards in a move that would have ramifications in Newcastle, but which was widely welcomed in the patriotic mood of the time. Local joint committees and joint shipyard committees were set up and these liaised with a national committee so that yards would be aware of future demands and could organize themselves and their labour accordingly. Given the boom in shipbuilding it was also unsurprising that a new company was created which purchased land at Hebburn in order to build a four berth facility for the building of ships.

The war had brought rewards to many industrial workers and with this had come an awareness of the importance of their efforts and sacrifices. This had awakened a growing interest in the Labour movement on Tyneside, and as a result of this an encouraged Labour Party declared that in the next election it would put up candidates in all four Newcastle seats (they already had one MP). The candidates reflected the predominantly heavy-engineering nature of the movement in Newcastle: Mr Walter Hudson, MP; Councillor David Adams, ship owner and metal merchant (ASE nominee); Councillor James Smith (ILP nominee); and Councillor G.J. Rowe (Tynemouth Boilermakers' official).

Newcastle's industrial base was irrevocably changed by the war with a number of the staple industries going into decline as the wartime boom ended. Due to the demands of the war, Newcastle-based industries had been dominated by the production of munitions. The war had created a quite artificial boom climate but the truth was that many of the factories, yards and workshops were outdated and had limited viable plans for a country at peace. This resulted in an almost immediate post-war slump which was only halted by the urgent need to build up the military once again in the mid-1930s.

A People's War?

Throughout January morale across the country sagged badly with the war news increasingly grim and people dejected after the costly failed offensives of 1917 and the capitulation of Russia which freed up many German troops for the Western Front. It was during this period that the government launched a new war bonds campaign to encourage the tired populace to contribute even more to the war effort. This met with mixed results but, again, Newcastle led the way. Government figures measuring the weekly contribution of the 'average' citizen of individual towns and cities demonstrate that the 'average' Newcastle citizen contributed over £22 over the fourteen week campaign period; the people of Newcastle contributed three times more than Oxford.[92] The reasons behind this generosity at this late stage of the war are unclear. Possible explanations could include large donations by wealthy individuals, but perhaps the most plausible is that many Newcastle workers were engaged in war work and as a result had experienced a boom throughout the war with an increase in living standards for a significant number and that this, combined with the genuine patriotism found in the city, explains their willingness to make such a financial sacrifice.

Although weary the people of Newcastle still demonstrated an incredible level of commitment towards the war effort and this was shown especially clearly in their willingness to contribute monetary donations in aid of the fighting forces, 1918 began with several fund raising campaigns. The most popular involved the establishment of a 'tank bank'. This involved people donating money to a tank parked in the city which had seen service on the

The use of a tank as a money raising symbol was hugely successful in Newcastle. The Women's Volunteer Corps were amongst those groups and individuals who bought War Saving's Certificates from the wounded servicemen who acted as collectors: Daily Mirror, 2 January 1918.

The Lord Mayor of Newcastle (Sir George Lunn) presents the Military Medal and Bar won for conspicuous gallantry and devotion to duty to Sergeant Stuttard: Daily Mirror, 27 August 1918.

Western Front. The generosity of the people was astounding and in one day £891,750 was raised, with £100,000 donated by the North-Eastern Railway Company. The total receipts of the 'tank bank' in Newcastle at this point stood at £1,802,874. In the first five days of the New Year the total raised was £2,374,924. Donations came from a wide range of participants; 500 soldiers marched through the city to the tank to purchase war savings certificates, a gentleman purchased a large number of bonds and distributed them to crippled children, a wounded soldier donated £3,000 and an orphan raised 15 shillings 6 pence to buy his first certificate. By the next day, the total raised had broken the £3,000,000 mark. Fund raising continued throughout January and February and by the end of the first week of February Newcastle stood a proud fourth in the war bonds table (behind only the much larger cities of Birmingham, Manchester and Liverpool) with the sum of £6,669,890 raised.

Newcastle tops lists for donations from provincial cities with fundraising efforts popularly supported throughout the war. In the words of historian Adrian Gregory, 'There seems to be a particular and peculiar Geordie patriotism being demonstrated'.[93] This is perhaps best explained by a number of factors: the dependency of the city on the munitions industries; the large number of Newcastle men serving abroad; the commemoration of the shattering losses in the Somme; and the traditionally pro-military nature of the city's residents.

Individuals also continued to make patriotic sacrifices and donations. Wealthy Newcastle ship owner and businessman Colonel C.H. Innes Hopkins of Ryton, donated his country mansion to the state for use as an orthopaedic hospital (particularly for the use of the Tyneside Scottish, Durham Light Infantry and Northumberland Fusiliers [in that order]) and once the war ended for use as a hospital for injured workers. Innes Hopkins had been a key player in the forming of the 'Tyneside Scottish' and had for a period commanded the unit before being forced to retire due to ill health. Recovering, he had served in France with the Devonshire Regiment before again being invalided home. Colonel Innes Hopkins had lost two sons in the war and asked that the hospital be dedicated to their memory.[94]

Fundraising continued right until the end of the war with a feed the guns campaign begun in October during the final push for victory. In Newcastle, great efforts were made to elicit the support of the population with pride of place going to the recreation of a battlefield scene complete with guns, dugouts and wire entanglements which was placed around the Boer War Memorial at the Haymarket in the city centre.

Concerns over the sometimes exorbitant food prices continued and were particularly evident throughout the first months of 1918. One Newcastle resident writing in *The Times* complaining over unfairness in the pricing of dates (which were popular amongst the working class of the district) and asking the food controller to investigate the matter. The correspondent claimed that the price of dates had increased by over 3 shillings in a week and that different shops were charging vastly differing prices for the same product. The writer also highlighted the growing disbelief of hardship amongst the traders amongst the people of the city.

The system of rationing that was enforced (in a piecemeal fashion) by the government met with a mixed response in Newcastle. The majority were in favour as they believed that it would lead to a fairer supply of food, but others resented the rationing, especially the meat ration introduced in April, as they believed that some local suppliers were profiteering and that they would flout the law in order to make even more money.

A further attempt to provide relief for those struggling with inflated food prices was the opening of a state restaurant in Newcastle. This provided nourishing food at a low price and a similar restaurant in London had been a great success. However, it was clear that such limited measures would be of little use in alleviating the worries of the many in Newcastle who were unable to provide sufficient sustenance for the families.

Against this backdrop of shortages, price rises and growing anxiety and discontent worries surfaced over the state of public morale in the country. A variety of tactics were used to try to maintain morale in the city including visits from dignitaries and politicians, meetings describing the work of the armed forces and extolling the contribution of Newcastle to the war effort (including fund-raising campaigns using aircraft and tanks). Always popular were meetings where the work of the flying services (the RFC [after 1 April, the RAF] and RNAS) were discussed. Such meetings were always well attended, perhaps because of the newness and the excitement that flying engendered in the Newcastle public. With the heavy engineering background of the city and the technical courses at Armstrong College many young students and engineers joined the RFC, the RNAS or the RAF. A number of members of the North-East Coast Institution of Engineers and Shipbuilders were in these services.

Patriotic fervour was further encouraged on Tyneside with a St George's Day message which highlighted the actions of Northumbrian troops in the recent heavy fighting at Picardy and Lys Valley. Five divisions, largely composed of Northumbrian troops, had taken a leading role in the fighting, while the 50th Northumbrian Division (again largely composed of local men) had been rushed to the front to reinforce the Portuguese after they had been heavily shelled. While this message did encourage the general populace it was also a source of great concern to the large numbers of Newcastle families with men serving in those units.

The visits of VIPs continued throughout the year as they were seen, usually rightly, as a good way of maintaining and boosting morale by ensuring that the people of the city felt involved and informed regarding the war and their part in it. One of the final such visits of the war came in September, as it was becoming increasingly clear that Germany was tottering and that while victory was in sight it would still be a hard struggle. It was during this month that General Jan Smuts paid another visit to Newcastle. Smuts visited the Mansion House and several shipyards giving speeches which emphasized that he was not in favour of jingoism but that the war was being fought for a good cause; a better future. His speech was a blatantly flattering one for his audience. He praised the region and the city by saying, 'I have always been told that if you want to see England, do not look at London, do not look at the flabby South. (Much laughter) Go north to the real centres of energy and industry. I have picked up fresh courage from what I have seen in your great town.' The speech was, of course, very well received and the visit was concluded with General Smuts being presented with the freedom of the city.[95]

The year also brought increased worries for many Newcastle households as men were 'combed out' of previously protected jobs for military service and the age for military service was repeatedly increased. In mid-April, all men under the age of 23 years 6 months who had been exempted from military service had their exemption cancelled. This was a bitter blow for a large percentage of these men who were conscientious objectors (many on religious grounds), but given the urgency of the situation in France, the measure had widespread support in Newcastle with letters to local newspapers commenting that it was not before time and considerable anger shown towards 'slackers'.

Even in the fifth year of the war, the people of Newcastle remained very proud of their men in uniform and combined to celebrate and commemorate those who had died as heroes. The funeral of Private David Latimer of the Royal Marine Light Infantry was attended by a huge crowd of 50,000 with the Lord Mayor giving a graveside eulogy. Private Latimer, who was killed during the Zeebrugge raid, was buried with full-military honours at All Saints' cemetery. Latimer had previously been a champion swimmer in Newcastle and had lived at 13 Victoria Place. He was just 18 years-old when he was killed.

While the working-class population of Newcastle bore dreadful losses, the middle and upper classes also lost sons, brothers and fathers during this last year of the war. Towards the end of April, a famed Newcastle name stood out in the casualty lists. It was reported that Major Algernon George Parsons, Royal Field Artillery, had been killed on 26 April. Major Parson was the only son of the famous engineer, the Honourable Sir Charles Parsons, and was himself a director of C.A. Parsons & Co Ltd. Major Parsons had been commissioned in 1906, before leaving the army three years later to join his father's company. At the declaration of war he rejoined the army and was sent to France in November 1914. Major Parsons saw varied wartime service and was for a period in 1916, attached to the experimental department of the RFC and developed several technical innovations. In November 1917, he was serving with his unit at Cambrai, France when he was severely wounded and on his recovery he re-assumed command of his battery in March 1918. Major Parsons was a member of the North-East Coast Institution of Engineers and Shipbuilders; a list of members shows that there were 144 serving as of 1917, many of them Newcastle residents or with business interests in the city.[96] A later volume lists 258 men from the institution who were serving in 1918 (many with the Royal Engineers, RFC [RAF], Royal Artillery or the RN). Many were wounded while some twenty-six were killed or died of wounds and many were the recipients of medals or other awards. Although Newcastle's industry was booming, the city could ill afford the loss of these educated men who would have played a large role in the development of industry in the city.

Far from being remote from the conflict many of the councillors and aldermen from Newcastle City Council served in the military and a large number lost their lives. The Lord Mayor, Sir George Lunn, for example, had three sons and a son-in-law serving in the King's African Rifles, the RFC (RAF), the 37th Infantry Brigade, and the King's Own Yorkshire Light Infantry. Alderman Kirby had two son-in-laws and seven grandsons in the military. Amongst those lost was a son-in-law, Surgeon General James Albert Clery who died in February 1920 (presumably of war-related injuries or illness as he is named on the Commonwealth War Graves Commission website). Clery's son, Noel was killed (serving as a captain in the Royal Field Artillery) in 1916. Alderman Sir Riley Lord had four grandsons serving and lost two: Captain Roland Lord was killed in October 1918, while serving with the 1st Battalion Northumberland Fusiliers; Flight Sub-Lieutenant Reginald Lord was killed on 10 August 1915, serving with the RNAS.

Flight Sub-Lieutenant Reginald Lord, Royal Naval Air Service, was the grandson of Lord Riley Lord of Felton Park, Newcastle, and son of the late Albert Lord of Highfield Hall, Newcastle. He was killed attempting to land in the dark after attacking a Zeppelin over Ostend. Tragically, Sub-Lieutenant Lord had been dancing with his fiancé just half an hour before his death. His three brothers were all serving in the Army: Daily Record, 12 August 1915.

With a large Irish population Newcastle was carefully observed by the authorities in case of the development of pro-Irish sympathies. The Irish question had become increasingly troubling following the Easter Rising of 1916 and it was thought by many on Tyneside that the Irish, and those of Irish descent who lived locally, could be a source of trouble but this was countered by the city's pride in the locally raised 'Tyneside Irish' brigade. The Home Rule campaign did indeed find powerful allies in Newcastle. In April, while the army in France was still struggling to halt the German offensive, a petition by 60,000 influential Irish men and women was sent to the Prime Minister. The petition called for immediate self government in Ireland and was championed by Colonel Joseph Cowen of Blaydon. A letter from local MP, Mr Thomas Burt, accompanied the petition and stated that as a dedicated Home Rule supporter he hoped that the Prime Minister was giving this matter his serious and urgent attention. The reply from the Prime Minister stated that he himself wished to see a speedy resolution, that he was sympathetic and that he was indeed taking the matter extremely seriously but that the problem was a difficult one to solve.[97]

Probably as a result of the recent German offensive and the Zeppelin raid on Durham and Hartlepool, which killed eight people, there was another outbreak of anti-alien feeling in the city during the summer of 1918. There were several meetings which urged the internment of all enemy aliens and there was suspicion that aliens were responsible for attempting subvert morale among workers and the army. A Russian woman, Julia Klasvosky, was charged with distributing a newspaper, The *Young Socialist* which, it was said, was likely to prejudice discipline in the army. Klasvosky was sentenced to two weeks in prison and was recommended for expulsion from Britain. Although called to strike, workers at Armstrong Whitworth passed a resolution to remain at work until further instruction could be sought from their executive and stating that German influence was the cause of the unrest in Newcastle and the country in general and called on the government to intern all Germans, especially those who worked in government, particularly the Department of Munitions. The anti-German feeling passed as far as the council when they agreed to support a resolution from Grimsby Council urging the internment of all enemy aliens, naturalized or not. Speaking in favour of the resolution Alderman Forster said that, 'he hoped that some action would be taken without delay. They had, he added, a lot of Hun blood about, and many ships had been lost through information having been passed on to the enemy from that and other ports'. The resolution was passed unanimously by the council, demonstrating the popular feeling of the time.[98] These measures were only part of a wave of similar resolutions with bakers in Newcastle also passing a resolution that no enemy alien be allowed to join their organization until twenty years after the war.

Among those who were not patriotically inclined the war, the mounting casualties and the grief of the many bereaved was a source for exploitation. Some of those who preyed on the bereaved were a number of fake fortune tellers who generally exploited women. In April, a case of fraudulent fortune telling was heard in Newcastle. Mary Darling Purvis was tried after telling the fortune of two police women who visited her. She told the officers that they would both do well after joining the WAAC and revealed many alleged details of events at the Front before she was arrested. Purvis was found guilty and fined the sum of £25.

The case also highlighted another function which women had taken on because of the war. Previously female police officers would have been unacceptable, but they were thought an effective deterrent when dealing with prostitution and the perceived decline in morale standards which resulted in the increase of crimes of an indecent nature amongst women. They were

Newcastle City Police, 1918. (Newcastle City Library)

particularly useful in monitoring venereal-disease rates among prostitutes. Clearly the above case demonstrates that these women were useful for advanced police work and that Newcastle City Police were quite willing to use women in their battle against wartime crime.

Many young women were also keen to become directly involved with the war effort. The formation of the Women's Auxiliary Army Corps (WAAC) in late March, proved very popular with a large percentage of the young women of Newcastle (despite higher wages being available for munitions work). The volunteers had varied reasons for deciding on joining the WAAC with some having lost family members in the fighting and others wishing to serve in uniform rather than working in a factory.

On 21 March, the offensive launched by the German Army saw the British Army forced to retreat in disarray and once again suffer heavy casualties. Clearly it was difficult to put a positive spin on this news and it was greeted in Newcastle with attitudes ranging from determination to dismay. Coincidentally, the offensive came at a time when yet another VIP tour of the city was announced; this time by General Jan Smuts on 12-13 April. General Smuts was to address a meeting of the National War Aims Committee and was also to be presented with the freedom of the city.

The contribution of women was, at times recognised. Matron Lottie Darley of the St. John Ambulance Brigade Auxiliary Hospital at Newcastle was awarded the Royal Red Cross (R.R.C.): Daily Mirror, 25 July 1918.

The continued German offensive was repeatedly downplayed in the press although to most careful Newcastle readers it was obvious that the situation was bleak. Despite this, the residents of Newcastle once again showed their fighting spirit and patriotism. The employers, union officials and workers in the heavy engineering, shipbuilding and munitions industries organized a large meeting at Bolbec Hall. The meeting was overwhelmingly patriotic in tone and the chairman sent a telegraph to the Prime Minister with the text of the resolution which was passed unanimously: 'this large and representative meeting of North-East Coast engineering, shipbuilding, and ship-repairing employers and trade union representatives have watched with pride and confidence the stirring deeds and unconquerable spirit of the British and Allied Armies on the Western Front. Spurred on by the glorious example of the fighting forces, the industrial force in the North-East Coast ordnance, shell, and aviation shops, engine works, shipyards and ship-repairing establishments assure their comrades in the fighting line that they will do everything in their power to turn out in increasing numbers guns, shells, engines, ships, and other munitions of war. Employers and workmen stand shoulder to shoulder, determined to maintain and increase their efforts until complete victory crowns our arms.'[199]

Even in the early summer, a widespread influenza epidemic hit the country in a ghastly foreshadowing of events to come. In Newcastle, hundreds were affected and the miners of Northumberland were so badly affected that production suffered greatly with a subsequent knock-on effect on the Newcastle coal-shipment trade. As the epidemic spread, it began to affect the productivity in the crucial armaments factories with munitions worker, who worked long hours in close proximity, badly affected; other groups to suffer included school children, teachers, nurses and medical students along with numbers of police and fire brigade. Thankfully, the vast majority of cases recovered quickly but the loss of productivity was of serious concern. Given the recent epidemic, the people of Newcastle were understandably nervous about health matters and when a Russian ship, with several persons suffering from smallpox on board, docked a mild panic gripped the city as rumours of an epidemic swept across the city. Thankfully, the cases had been isolated on the ship and those unfortunates were quickly rushed to hospital in the city and placed in isolation while the crew were quarantined.

In October, influenza again became a worrying problem when the situation was so serious that measures were taken to ban some groups from attending popular entertainment venues. The young were particularly affected with school lessons being cancelled and school age children forbidden from attending the cinema.

Football was quickly re-established in time for the 1919/20 season but, like other clubs, Newcastle United had to completely rebuild. Several players had been killed in the war and others wounded while many had joined other clubs or retired. The influenza epidemic also had an effect on the club with Angus Douglas returning to St James' only to die from the disease in December 1918. A former favourite Bobby Templeton and Stan Allen, a former reserve centre forward, died in Newcastle as a result of the epidemic.[100]

During the course of the war, the price of beer trebled and the strength of beer was decreased equally dramatically but it became clear at the end of the war that the measures had not been entirely effective as, despite consumption of beer being significantly down, the consumption of strong spirits had increased by 40 per cent. There was still a great deal of anger among the workers directed towards the brewers and those who sought to control the consumption of alcohol. Statements from drinkers regarding the beer served in Newcastle, described the brewers as thieves who were as 'light fingered as their ales are light' while others criticized the quality as being 'not fit for hogwash.'[101] At the end of the war, the consumption quickly rose before falling again as the post-war depression bit.

Notes

87   Moffat & Rosie: *Tyneside*, pp. 305.

88   Vall. Natasha: *The Emergence of the Post-Industrial Economy in Newcastle 1914-2000*, in Colls, R & Lancaster. B: *Newcastle upon Tyne. A Modern History* (2001), pp. 49-51.

89   Moffat & Rosie: *Tyneside*, pp. 308.

90   Vall. Natasha: *The Emergence of the Post-Industrial Economy in Newcastle 1914-2000*, in Colls, R & Lancaster. B: *Newcastle upon Tyne. A Modern History* (2001), pp. 49-50.

91   Hinton. J: *The First Shop Stewards' Movement* (1973), pp. 189.

92   Gregory. Adrian: *The Last Great War. British Society and the First World War* (2008), pp. 223-225.

93   Gregory. Adrian: *The Last Great War* (2008).

94   They were 27 year-old Private Castell Percy Innes Hopkins, 9th Battalion, Gordon Highlanders, killed on 25 September 1915, commemorated on the Loos Memorial and 21 year-old Lieutenant Charles Randolph Innes Hopkins, 2nd Battalion, Cameronians (Scottish Rifles), killed on 18 December 1914, buried at the Royal Irish Rifles Graveyard, Laventie.

95   *The Times*, 14 September 1918, pp. 8.

96   TWAM: AS.IES/3/1/26. North-East Coast Institution of Engineers & Shipbuilders, Lists of Members, 13 February 1917

97   *The Times*, 3 May 1918, pp. 7.

98   Ibid, 1 August 1918, pp. 3.

99   *The Times*, 6 April 1918, pp. 3.

100 Joannu. Paul: *United*, pp. 110.

101 Bennison. Brian: 'Drink in Newcastle', in *Newcastle upon Tyne. A Modern History* (2001), pp. 178.

Chapter 6

Peace and Commemoration

Approaching Newcastle city centre from the north, the scene is dominated by the church of St Thomas' and by the massive form of the war memorial entitled 'The Response' in the old churchyard. The memorial consists of a bronze sculpture mounted on pink granite and stands approximately 30ft high and 23ft wide. The bronze portrays men of Newcastle marching off to war in 1914, led by either winged victory or an angel blowing a horn. The memorial was primarily dedicated to the men who joined the 'Tyneside Commercial' battalion. The men are in early-war uniform with some in part civilian dress and unusually the sculpture also shows the women and children they left behind. One soldier is bidding farewell to his wife, while one has his rifle carried by his son and another carries his father's kit bag. The reverse of the monument portrays St George between two shields and the motto of the Northumberland Fusiliers *Quo Fata Vocant* (wherever the fates call) and to the sides are two fusiliers; one portrayed in the uniform when the regiment formed in 1674 and the other wearing 1914-1918 uniform.[102] Although Adrian Gregory implies that the memorial is triumphalist in tone, I believe that it portrays the civic pride that the people of Newcastle had in the epic response of the men of the city, mixed with a wish to portray the sacrifice not only of those who served but also of the families who were left behind. It is exceptionally rare to find a war memorial portraying the wives and children of soldiers and, despite Gregory's claim that the memorial is triumphalist because of the figure of winged victory (and it is debatable whether that is the correct interpretation of the figure), I find the memorial moving and poignant.[103]

The memorial was commissioned by Sir George and Lady Renwick at a cost of almost £3,000. The Renwick's saw five sons go off to war and all five returned safely. Sir George had traded on the Quayside for fifty years; the memorial was dedicated to these two events and the raising of the 'Tyneside Commercials'. The memorial bears the inscription; 'To commemorate the raising of the B. Coy 9th Batt. & the 16th, 18th and 19th Service Battalions Northumberland Fusiliers, by the Newcastle and Gateshead Chamber of Commerce Aug-Oct. 1914.' The man leading the response is said to have been modelled on Sir George himself.[104]

The attention to details on the sculpting is superb and even extends to the men being armed differently. When the 'Tyneside Commercials' were raised there was initially a shortage of weapons and the memorial therefore accurately shows some of the men with the standard Lee-Enfield infantry rifle

A photo of George Renwick (later Sir George) taken in 1900. Sir George saw his sons return safely from the war and paid for the war memorial 'The Response' after the war. (Newcastle City Library)

and other with the short-magazine version. There is anecdotal evidence that several of the figures portrayed were modelled on actual people including the two drummer boys who are said to have been modelled on two soldiers who survived the war. There was some disagreement over the siting of the memorial as its current positioning shows the winged figure leading the men to the north, away from the railway station.[105] This could be explained by the fact that the initial training of the battalion took place at Alnwick which is to the north. The monument was unveiled by HRH the Prince of Wales on 5 July 1923. Money was raised to thoroughly clean the memorial before a re-dedication service, attended by the Duke of Edinburgh and several members of the Renwick family, was held on 25 October 2007.

At the end of the war, Newcastle could reflect on the vast number of men it had lost. Without a doubt the worst single day had been the 1 July 1916, but there were others which had also seen massive loss of life from the city. Families, of course, had their own personal grief and ways of mourning but, in common with other areas, Newcastle was keen to commemorate the men (and women) it had lost in the war.

Loss rates from businesses, clubs and organization varied considerably with those which had seen large numbers of men joining the 'pals' battalions suffering the worst. For example, 714 former employees of the Newcastle and Gateshead Gas Company served during the war with seventy men being killed; a loss rate of 9.8 per cent. The workers of the North Eastern Railway Company based at the company's Heaton Junction Depot also had a strong record of enlistment with over 20 per cent of the workforce joining up; over 15 per cent of those who served were lost. One of those NER volunteers, Regimental Sergeant Major Albert E. Pollard, was awarded with the Military Medal while serving with the 6/7th Battalion of the Royal Scots Fusiliers. The paper merchants, R. Robinson Co. Ltd. of Clavering Place, lost over 10 per cent of its ninety-six employees, while Newcastle breweries lost at least thirteen men.

Sporting clubs and religious organizations were also badly affected with high average loss rates. The losses were commemorated in a variety of ways including the creation of memorial cups and sports competitions to the more standard form of memorial. The Heaton Temperance Amateur Cycling Club, for example, had thirty-eight members who served (including two women who served in the WAAC.) and lost four (11 per cent). The Heaton based Bohemians Association Football Club seem to have been particularly unlucky having lost at least eight players or former players

The Response. (Newcastle City Library)

from at least thirty-three who served (24 per cent). The randomness of casualties is shown by the losses of a neighbouring football club. Heaton Stannington had fifty-four members serving during the war and only three were killed.

Schools were also determined to commemorate former pupils and staff who had made the ultimate sacrifice. Almost every Newcastle school lost someone and subsequently commissioned a plaque to mark the sacrifice. Westgate Road Council School, for example, commissioned a copper plaque commemorating the fifty-five former pupils killed during the war. The dead included Able Seaman John William Blakey (killed aged 21 years-old in March 1917, serving on HMS *Paragon*) and his brother Charles (killed in April 1918 serving with 18th Northumberland Fusiliers). Other brothers included Private Charles Reginald Goodhall (killed aged 19 years-old in March 1917, with 22nd Royal Fusiliers) and his older brother Ship's Steward Gerald Arthur (killed aged 24 years-old in January 1915, while serving on HMS *Viknor*). There are also two Smiths recorded (including Sergeant Leigh Smith of C Battery, 72nd Brigade, Royal Field Artillery; killed aged 28 years-old in August 1918), but it has proven impossible to discover if they were related.

Very sadly, many of the memorials have gone missing, been relocated or, in some cases, shamefully sold or destroyed. The Cuthbert Bainbridge Memorial Wesleyan Methodist church which once stood on Heaton Road, for example, had six stained-glass windows commissioned in remembrance of fallen members of those 179 men with connections to church who served. Two windows commemorated the twenty-three men of the congregation who fell while four others commemorated individuals (Lieutenant Arthur Victor Knox, Northumberland Fusiliers; Lieutenant John Charles Pearson Barkas, Durham Light Infantry; Lance Corporal James Fenwick Moore, Northumberland Fusiliers; and Rifleman Arthur E. Murray, London Regiment (Post Office Rifles). The church has since been demolished and replaced with sheltered accommodation but, thankfully, the windows have been incorporated into the new building. There was also a commemorative plaque in the church which is now apparently in storage. The plaque commemorating those men who were

At the end of the war Newcastle's contribution was recognised during a visit by the Prime Minister, Lloyd George, and other members of the government (Winston Churchill is on the right of the photograph): Daily Mirror, 30 November 1918.

Blaydon war memorial. (Newcastle City Library)

lost from the Royal Insurance Co., (which had offices on Grey Street), was moved to the Midlands and is now in storage at the Royal National Arboretum. It is known that Parsons had an extensive roll of honour in their Heaton works on Shields Road, but after the building was demolished in the 1950s the memorial has disappeared. The company Angus Watson & Co. had eighty-seven employees who served during the war and fourteen of these men were killed (almost 14 per cent). The plaque which commemorated these men has subsequently been lost after the building was demolished.

Other memorials have been neglected or left in basements and cellars to steadily be destroyed by the passage of time. Thankfully, some have recently been recovered and restored. In 1984, a paper memorial behind glass was discovered in the basement of Pilgrim Street police station. The scroll was an extensive list of those family members of the city council who had served during the war. It catalogued 135 men who had served along with their rank and regiment. From it we can see that the families of council members served extensively.

The men who had survived the war slowly returned to Newcastle but found that the war had changed the city and themselves. Many, in common with other veterans, found it hard to open up about their experiences overseas and instead turned to the newly-created veterans' organizations such as the Royal British Legion. With the building of the many memorials in Newcastle during the immediate post-war years, attendances at commemorations on 11 November remained extremely high with veterans keen to remember their fallen comrades. In Newcastle, the main ceremony took place at the war memorial built at Old Eldon Square. There were a number of proposals for how Newcastle should commemorate those lost in the war. The new Lord Mayor, Mr A. Munro Sutherland, proposed the building of a new city hall which would cost £500,000; while the candidate for Benwell Ward suggested that an international exhibition be held each year. These were turned down and a shilling fund to raise money for a statue memorial was inaugurated. The Lord Mayor donated £1,000 and the general public enthusiastically rallied to the cause and by January 1921 had raised a further £15,000. The memorial of St George and the Dragon (St George features on the badge of the Northumberland Fusiliers) was the second cast from a design to commemorate the men of Marylebone and is identical to a memorial which stands close to Lord's Cricket Ground. On 26 September, the memorial was unveiled by Earl Haig in front of a large crowd. Sadly, the memorial was not always widely respected and it was vandalized in 1990 but restored a year later. A planned development of the square in the early 1990s would have resulted in the removal of the memorial. The proposal greatly angered the people of Newcastle and the subsequent public outcry led to the abandonment of the plan. The inscription on the memorial reads:

1914-1918
1939-1945
A tribute of affection
to the men of
Newcastle and District
who gave their lives
in the cause of freedom
Their name liveth for evermore

Memory lingers here

Eldon Square before the construction of the city's war memorial. (Newcastle City Library)

Stained glass windows and plaques in St Barnabas Church, Jesmond, in memoriam of 2nd Lieutenant Henry Adolph Lung, killed aged 21 whilst serving with the 1st Battalion Northumberland Fusiliers in May 1915 and Lance Corporal George Swan. (Newcastle City Library)

Notes

102 North East War Memorials Project website [http://www.newmp.org.uk/detail.php?contentId=10944], accessed 20/09/2013.

103 Gregory. Adrian: *The Last Great War. British Society and the First World War* (2008), pp. 268.

104 North East War Memorials Project website [http://www.newmp.org.uk/detail.php?contentId=10944], accessed 20/09/2013.

105 Ibid.

CHAPTER 7

The Sacrifice

1914

Boy First Class Adam Flockhart, RN: HMS *Hawke*, 15 October 1914.
Numbered among those who were under 18 years-old when they lost their
lives in the war was Boy First Class Adam Flockhart Adam he was killed
aged 17 years-old was the son of John and Margaret Flockhart of 29 Prudhoe
Street, Newcastle upon Tyne. He was among the crew of HMS *Hawke*, an
old and out-dated Edgar-class protected cruiser launched in 1891. HMS
Hawke had been paid off the strength and transferred to the Fleet Reserve
in 1901, but continued in service off the Cape of Good Hope. During the
war the ship was commanded by Captain Hugh Williams and was engaged
in a variety of operations in the North Sea. The old cruiser was primarily
used for training and so its complement included a large number of cadets
and reservists. Opinion after the sinking questioned whether vessels such
as HMS *Hawke* were fit for active service of any kind. On 15 October, the
ship was cruising off the east coast of Scotland in company with her sister
ship HMS *Theseus*. The *Hawke* had just rendezvoued with HMS *Endymion*
to collect mail but, unknown to the ships' crews, the German submarine
U-9 was stalking them. U-9 had already become infamous as the submarine
which, a month previously, had sunk three British cruisers (HMS *Aboukir*,
HMS *Hogue* and HMS *Cressy*). The submarine fired a torpedo at HMS
Theseus but missed and instead hit *Hawke*. The torpedo ignited a magazine
and resulted in a massive explosion which blew the ship apart with the

wreckage sinking in minutes. Captain Williams, twenty-six officers and 497 men (including Adam Flockhart) were lost and of the 594 men on board only 70 survived. Adam is commemorated on the Portsmouth Naval Memorial to those with no known grave and also on the St Thomas' School Memorial Plaque in Newcastle.

Private Thomas William Robson: Royal Marine Light Infantry, 5 September 1914.

Thomas Robson was the son of Mr and Mrs J.L. Robson of 89 Carville Road, Byker and had served for two years in the Royal Navy before the war. After leaving the navy he had enlisted as a territorial in the Royal Marine Light Infantry.[106] He was lost when HMS *Pathfinder* was sunk and is commemorated on the Chatham Naval Memorial.

Captain Hugh Taylor, Scots Guards, was a native of Newcastle (his father lived at Chipchase Castle) who was Unionist candidate for Sunderland before the war. He was declared killed in action on Christmas Day leaving behind a widow and two children: Newcastle Journal, 29 December 1914.

1915

Lieutenant Colonel Lord Ninian Edward Crichton-Stuart: 6th Battalion, Welsh Regiment, 2 October 1915.
N.E. Crichton-Stuart was a member of the North East Institute of Mining & Mechanical Engineers. He lived in Fife and was the Conservative MP for Cardiff. The second son of the third Marquis of Bute, N.E. Crichton-Stuart was on the reserve list of officers and was called up at the start of the war. Lord Crichton-Stuart fought throughout 1914-1915 and, aged just 32, was commanding the 6th Battalion, Welsh Regiment in the closing stages of the Battle of Loos when a fellow officer was wounded and cut off by the enemy. Crichton-Stuart led a counter charge in an attempt to rescue the wounded officer but during this assault he was shot in the head and killed.

Lieutenant John Powe Roberts: 9th Battalion, Australian Infantry, 26 August 1915.
John Roberts was born in Newcastle as the seventh child of Arthur and Jessie. Part of a large family John had at least ten brothers and sisters and three half-brothers or sisters. In 1904, John married Sarah Mallen and in 1911 was working as a plumber living at Armstrong Street in Dunston. A freemason with the degree of master mason, John and his family decided to immigrate to Australia and he left along with his younger brother, Septimus, from Liverpool in the summer of 1911. The family settled in North Ipswich, Queensland where he found employment as a sanitary engineer. As he had previously served for twelve years in the Durham Light Infantry, at the declaration of war he joined the Australian Army and was given a commission.

In 1915, Mallen and his battalion were part of the Gallipoli campaign. He was killed at some date between 25 and 28 August and although it seems that his body was recovered and buried but the location was lost. John Mallen is commemorated, along with twenty-five others, on a special memorial at Walker's Ridge Cemetery, Anzac.

Private Thomas ('Tommie') Lancelot Gawain: B Company, 1st Battalion, Honourable Artillery Company, 15 April 1915.
Although born in London, 'Tommie' Gawain was a partner in the Turnbull, Scott & Co. shipping firm and a member of the Baltic Exchange. Both he and his brother volunteered for the army. He was described as being cheerful and well liked by his colleagues. Gawain was severely

wounded in action near Ypres, aged 22 years-old, and subsequently died of his wounds on 15 April 1915. He is buried at Dickebusch New Military Cemetery.

1916

Corporal James Ballantyne: 16th Battalion, Northumberland Fusiliers, 1 July 1916

In 1914, Glasgow-born James Ballantyne, was working as a draper in Newcastle and, when his company called for volunteers to join the army, he immediately joined the 16th Northumberland Fusiliers (1st 'Tyneside Commercials'). Rapidly promoted to corporal, he was sent to France with his unit in November 1915. The 'Tyneside Commercials' were deployed for the attack on Thiepval on the first day of the Somme. Ballantyne went over the top with his men during the advance. Apparently he was wounded, as he was seen leaving a dressing station, but after that he was not seen again and could not subsequently be traced. James Ballantyne was obviously a very highly valued NCO as his commanding officer wrote, 'such a capable and hard working NCO who, by his coolness under fire, won the respect of all his men'.[107]

He was 22 years-old at the time of his death and because his body was not found he is commemorated on the Thiepval Memorial. He is also commemorated at the Jesmond United Reform Church (then the John Knox Presbyterian Church), where his parents were members.

Second Lieutenant Percy George Hall: 23rd Battalion ('Tyneside Scottish'), Northumberland Fusiliers, 30 June 1916.

The son of a Newcastle JP (his mother had died in 1912) Percy Hall had grown up at 2 Haldane Terrace and was a member of the John Knox Presbyterian Church where his father was an elder of the church. Hall led a short but active life and on leaving Newcastle Grammar School in 1909, he signed up for a voyage to Australia on the Cadet School Ship Port Jackson. After returning he decided upon a career at sea and subsequently served an apprenticeship on ocean-going sailing ships. During August 1914, his vessel narrowly escaped a German raider en-route to Australia. Returning to England in 1915, he was offered a commission in the 'Tyneside Scottish' Marked out for future promotion he attended a course at Staff College before shipping out to France in January 1916.

The 'Tyneside Scottish' were slated to mount an assault on La Boiselle, but two days before the attack the British realized that not all the enemy wire had been destroyed and that engineers would have to go out at night to destroy the wire before the attack could take place. A call went round for volunteers from Second Lieutenant Hall's battalion to form a covering party. Hall and twenty men volunteered and set out from the trenches at around midnight but he was shot and killed by a sniper. His parent's received a letter praising him for his courage and it was said that Second Lieutenant Hall was to lead the attack the next day as his CO believed, 'nothing but a rifle bullet would stop Lieutenant Hall and his men would follow him anywhere.'[108]

Percy Hall was 23 years-old when he was killed and his body is buried at the Albert Communal Cemetery Extension.

Captain Harold Price, MC: 26th Battalion (3rd 'Tyneside Irish'), Northumberland Fusiliers, 26 June 1916.

Harold Price was born and educated in Vancouver, British Columbia, Canada, and had attended McGill University before becoming a land surveyor. He was in England at the outbreak of war and immediately volunteered as a private in the Royal Fusiliers. After training he was gazetted as a captain and posted to the 'Tyneside Irish' as battalion adjutant. Unhappy with this role, Price resigned as adjutant but carried on as a company commander. During his time with the 'Tyneside Irish', he became an active member of the John Knox Presbyterian Church congregation and regularly attended services.

After reaching France, Captain Price quickly proved himself in action and was twice mentioned in dispatches before being awarded the Military Cross for various acts of courage. In the build up to the Somme offensive, Price was ordered to command a trench raid but on his return to British lines discovered that one of his men was missing. He immediately returned to no-mans land to search for the missing man but was killed.

Captain Roy Craig Dunford, DSO: 1/6th Battalion, Northumberland Fusiliers.

Roy Dunford was born at Kirkcudbright, Scotland on 7 June 1881. He moved to Newcastle, and set up his own business as a chartered accountant at St Nicholas Chambers after being articled to Messrs J.M. Winter & Sons. Dunford was also a freemason (Golfers' Lodge, Freemasons Hall, Grainger Street) and a keen golfer being a member of Northumberland Golf Club, Gosforth.

He was commissioned in the 1/6th Battalion, Northumberland Fusiliers, and was promoted to captain sometime before his posting to France in September 1915. During that year he was slightly wounded and returned home to recuperate. In January 1916, Dunford returned to his unit in France and served throughout that year being awarded a DSO for his courage in action, there are unconfirmed rumours that he was in fact recommended for the Victoria Cross. In late 1916, he was severely injured in the course of his unit's action at High Wood on the Somme and was evacuated home for treatment. Captain Roy Dunford died of his wounds on the 10 November and was subsequently buried in Old Jesmond General Cemetery.

Corporal Lindsay Nelson Stephens: B Company, 9th Battalion, Northumberland Fusiliers, 6 May 1916.

Newcastle-born Lindsay Nelson was the son of Richard and Alice Stephens of Abbey Hurst, Corbridge. He attended the Royal Grammar School and after worked in the shipping industry. When war was declared, he immediately volunteered and became a private in the 9th Northumberland Fusiliers and subsequently posted to France in June 1915. Stephens was quickly promoted to corporal and saw a great deal of service. On 6 May 1916, he was involved in wiring-laying duties in front of the lines. Corporal Stephens was killed by machine-gun fire.

It transpired that Corporal Lindsay had given such good service that his commanding officer had decided to recommend him for a commission in recognition. Corporal Stephens was aged 20 or 21 years-old at the time of his death. He is buried at Armentieres.

1917

Private Lawrence John Nicholson: 2nd Battalion, The Duke of Edinburgh's (Wiltshire Regiment), 9 April 1917.

Private Nicholson was the only son of John and Emily Nicholson of 10 Woodbine Road, Gosforth. He was born at Newcastle and is listed as residing in the city but enlisted in the Royal Sussex Regiment at Mansion Houses, Middlesex before later being rebadged as a Wiltshire: presumably after being wounded. He was killed in action on the first day of the Battle of Arras on 9 April aged 23 years-old. A part of this action was the First Battle of the Scarpe which took place from 9 to 14 April. A crucial part of

The Grobe, Gosforth, was the pre-war home of Lieutenant Brewis. (Newcastle City Library)

the battle plan was the taking of the heavily-fortified village of Neuville-Vitasse. This had remained largely in German hands until an attack by the 56th (London) Division succeeded on 11 April. Private Nicholson lost his life during an assault by elements of his 30th Division on the village by the 56th (London) Division. He is buried in the Neuville-Vitasse Road Cemetery. This cemetery is small by First World War standards and contains only eighty-six graves. The cemetery was dug by the troops of the 33rd Division after the attack on 9 April. Apart from two burials in June 1917, the cemetery contains the bodies of Private Nicholson's comrades killed during the First Battle of the Scarpe.

In addition to his Commonwealth War Graves Commission headstone, Private Nicholson is commemorated by a stained-glass window at St Nicholas' Parish Church, Gosforth. The window was paid for by his parents and depicts an archangel at Christ's tomb and bears the inscription: 'To the Glory of God and in loving memory of Lawrence John Nicholson of Gosforth born August 15, 1893 who gave his life for his country and fell near Arras, France 1917. "Greater love hath no man than this"'. The window is accompanied by a brass plaque giving details of Private Nicholson's service experience.

Lieutenant John Arthur Gardner Brewis: No 40 Squadron (Royal Flying Corps), 29 April 1917.

J.A.G. Brewis was born in Sheffield in 1895 but was brought up in the Newcastle area. By 1901, his parents John Gardner and Florence Mary lived at 'Glengarriffe', The Grove, Gosforth. He was their only son and had four sisters. His father was an importer of foreign produce and/or butter. It seems that John was keen on a career within the army as the *London Gazette* of 21 August 1914 lists him among the cadets and ex-cadets of the Officer's Training Corps to be commissioned. At first Brewis was listed as serving with the 4th Battalion, Durham Light Infantry (DLI). By the time he was posted to France on 12 May 1915, he was a Second Lieutenant with the 2nd Battalion DLI.

After transferring to the RFC and completing his pilot training, Lieutenant Brewis became a member of 40 Squadron, flying offensive operations in Nieuport 17 aircraft. This squadron was one of the most successful on the Western Front during the period. For the last month of his service, Brewis would have been a messmate of the man who would go on to become the most successful British fighter pilot of the war, Major (then Second Lieutenant) Edward Mannock.

Supporting the army during the Battle of Arras, the month of April 1917 was to become infamous in the RFC as 'Bloody April' due to the number of casualties suffered due to outdated aircraft and poor tactics. The average lifespan of a pilot dropped to just seventeen days and the RFC lost almost a third of its strength in the month: 151 aircraft and 316 airmen; one of whom was John Brewis. Indeed, the date on which Brewis was killed has been called the 'awesome climax' to 'Bloody April'.[109]

On Tuesday, 24 April, at around midday Brewis and two colleagues, Ian P.R. Napier of 40 Squadron (who went on to become an ace with twelve victories) and Flight Sub-Lieutenant Robert A. Little of 8 Squadron RNAS (who went on to become Australia's highest-scoring ace with forty-seven victories before he was killed in May 1918), were responsible for driving down an enemy DFW C.V two-seat reconnaissance aircraft; the DFW was forced to land in British lines just northeast of Oppy after being intercepted at between 12,000 and 17,000ft.[110]

At 06:45am on the morning of Sunday, 29 April, Lieutenant Brewis took off on a morning patrol in Nieuport 17 (A6739). During the course of the patrol he was shot down by 'Archie' (anti-aircraft fire north) of Hendecourt. Two anti-aircraft unit s(Flak 61 and 62)[111] claimed to have shot-down his aircraft. Brewis was subsequently posted missing believed killed. In his will

Lieutenant Brewis left the sum of £328 7 shillings (over £15,000 today) to his father. John A.G. Brewis has no known grave and is one of the some 1,000 men commemorated on the Arras Flying Services Memorial.

Lieutenant John Halifax Feggetter, MC: 12th/13th Battalion, Northumberland Fusiliers, 4 October 1917.

John Feggetter was the son of William, a ship owner, and Amelia of 9 Dilston Terrace, Gosforth. He was born on 16 June 1895 and educated at Rutherford College then Armstrong College (to where he matriculated in 1914), to study English and Latin. A member of the John Knox Presbyterian Church, he was a teacher and the treasurer at the Sunday school. He was also a member of the Durham University Officer Training Corps and was commissioned in December 1915. From June 1916, he served in France and Flanders including extensive service on the Somme. On 13 July, he was wounded at Mametz Wood and was invalided home. On his recovery, Lieutenant Feggetter was made signalling officer and rejoined his regiment. In April 1917, he took part in an attack with his battalion to capture an enemy trench and led his signallers across open ground which was under heavy bombardment and machine-gun fire. On reaching the trench he quickly established communications and reorganized his men in order to hold the trench despite a heavy artillery and trench-mortar barrage. On another occasion, Feggetter led a patrol into no-man's land to pick up wounded. The official citation stated that he helped rescue, 'a great number of wounded men from near the enemy's wire.' For his actions, Lieutenant Feggetter was awarded the Military Cross.

Lieutenant Feggetter was a popular officer and his senior officers stated that his men would follow him anywhere and that his courage under fire was magnificent. A fellow officer commented in a letter home after Feggetter's death that it was 'a glorious end to a magnificent life.'[112] On 4 October 1917, Lieutenant Feggetter was part of his battalions attack and went forward alongside his commanding officer, Lieutenant Colonel Dix, acting as intelligence officer. During the course of the attack, both Lieutenant Feggetter and Lieutenant Colonel Dix were killed. It was said that Dix thought very highly of Feggetter. His death was keenly felt not only by the men of his own battalion, but also by men in the 'Queens' with which he had frequently been in contact.[113]

It transpired that Lieutenant Feggetter had been killed at Broodseinde and he was initially buried 100yd northwest of Reutel. His grave was not found after the war, but he is commemorated on panels nineteen to twenty-three and 162 of the Tyne Cot Memorial, Passendale and on eight separate memorials in Newcastle.

Signaller William Robert Lowe: HM Yacht *Verona,* Royal Navy Volunteer Reserve, 24 February 1917.

William Lowe was educated at Allan's Endowed School and in civilian life was a qualified chartered accountant. He volunteered for service at the beginning of March 1916 and joined the Tyneside Division of the RNVR and was trained as a signaller. In December, he was posted to the converted motor yacht, *Verona.* The vessel was used on mine-sweeping duties and William Lowe died on 24 February 1917, when *Verona* struck a mine in the North Sea and sank.

Lowe was 31 years-old when he was killed and he is commemorated on the Chatham Naval Memorial.

1918

Sergeant Thomas Alexander Gordon, MM: 16th Northumberland Fusiliers, 1 February 1918.

Thomas Gordon was the second son of four born to William and Hannah Gordon of 25 Sopwith Street, Benwell, Newcastle upon Tyne. Like many, he came from an industrial background as his father worked at the Elswick engineering works as a furnace man. He did not follow in his father's footsteps, and by 1914 was working as a tailor's cutter in the clothing department of the Newcastle Co-Operative Society.

He enlisted in the 16th (Service) Battalion in September 1914, shortly after the declaration of war as one of the last recruits to the battalion. This is confirmed by his service number: 16/701. His decision to join up may have been due to pressing family concerns as he had recently married and his wife, Edith was heavily pregnant.

On reaching France, the battalion was rapidly moved up to the Thiepval section of the Somme Sector and it was clear that operational security was not very good as they were greeted by cries of 'Hello Northumberlands' from the German trenches. The 16th quickly settled into the routine of trench life with duties at the Front, in support or in reserve, as working parties or training for the offensive which was obviously in preparation. The 16th were slated for an important role during the first day of the Somme. The 96th Brigade, of which the 16th

Battalion were a part, was tasked with the attack on the heavily-fortified village of Thiepval. Gordon's 'C' Company was positioned in support of the two leading companies ('A' and 'B'). His platoon, commanded by a sergeant who had joined up just after himself, suffered horrendous casualties including five killed and twenty-two wounded. The 16th as a whole suffered very badly and on the day following only eight officers and 279 other ranks were fit for duty.

By 1917, he had been promoted to corporal and in September of that year was awarded the Military Medal. Unfortunately, the medal did not come with a citation so it is not known what exactly why it was awarded; family tradition has it that he had carried a wounded officer back to British lines. Just two months later, he had been promoted to sergeant, and with the battalion due to move to the Ypres Salient in Belgium, he was given home leave for the Christmas period. It appears that this was the first time that he met his son, William, who was now 3 years-old. By January, Gordon was back with his battalion which was now in the dangerous Poelcappelle section of the Line. The battalion was holding the right-hand sector across the Staden railway and on the night of 1/2 February saw a company relief manoeuvre (with 'A' relieving 'B' while 'C' relieved 'D'). According to the battalion war diary, shortly after this relief had been carried out a 'Battle Patrol under Second Lieutenant Brownrigg made a determined attack on an enemy post near Turenne Crossing and succeeded in entering the post. But the Germans had withdrawn to two pill-boxes close at hand from which a heavy fire was opened on the patrol. A further attack on the pill-boxes was attempted but the fire was too close and accurate, and the patrol withdrew with the loss of two killed and one wounded. All the casualties were successfully brought back.' Tragically, Gordon was one of the two men killed. Five days later, the 16th Battalion was disbanded.[114]

His body was, it seems, recovered but unfortunately, like so many, the burial site was later lost or destroyed and so Thomas Gordon has no known grave but is commemorated on Panel nineteen to twenty-three and 162 of the Tyne Cot Memorial in Belgium.

Second Lieutenant William Burnett Row: 5th (Territorial) Battalion, The Prince of Wales' Own (West Yorkshire Regiment), 14 April 1918.
William Row born on 29 October 1897, was the eldest son of Henry and Mary who lived at 3 Windsor Terrace, South Gosforth. He was educated at

Rutherford College before entering an apprenticeship with Messrs Ainsley & Company, plumbers and electrical engineers. In May 1914, he joined the Territorial branch of the RAMC and at the beginning of the war he was attached to the Northern Cyclists Battalion responsible for patrolling and guarding the coast.

In November 1917, William Row was gazetted as a Second Lieutenant in the West Yorkshire Regiment and on 11 January 1918 he was posted to France. In the spring of 1918, his unit was occupying the lines near Bailleul when the Germany Army launched the Battle of the Lys as part of their 'Spring Offensive'. On 14 April, William Row was killed during fierce fighting near Meteren, one of 82,000 British casualties suffered in the battle from 9 to 30 April. He is buried at the Bailleul Communal Cemetery Extension, Nord. It is clear that he was held in high regard as an officer in his unit was recorded as saying that his fellow officers 'thought the world of him' while a sergeant claimed he had never met a braver officer.

Lieutenant John Pittendrigh: HMS *Hussar*, RNR, 28 October 1918.
Pittendrigh was born in Aberdeen and later lived at 165 Osborne Road, Jesmond. In pre-war years, Lieutenant Pittendrigh was an officer in the merchant marine and in 1914 was studying for his master's certificate. He answered the call for volunteers for naval service and was posted as a gunnery officer to the armed-boarding steamer HMS *Sarnia*. During his service on this ship, he saw active service at the Dardanelles and he was beach officer during the evacuation of Suvla Bay. After his service in the Dardanelles, Pittendrigh was posted to the armoured cruiser HMS *Drake* where he served from May 1916 until April 1917.

In August 1917, he was promoted as Senior Gunnery Lieutenant on HMS *Hussar*, a Dryad-class torpedo gunboat. The ship was patrolling off Italy in October 1918, when an epidemic of influenza broke out on the ship which Pittedrigh caught. On 28 October, he died aged 28 years-old and is buried at Genoa.[115]

Lieutenant Gilbert Atkinson: 8th Battalion, Durham Light Infantry, 4 October 1918.
Gilbert Atkinson was a native of Stocksfield-on-Tyne and his parents resided in Newcastle at 86 St George's Terrace. He was educated at the Universities of Glasgow and Edinburgh and was a member of staff

in the Faculty of Commerce at Newcastle College where he lectured in accountancy. In addition to his lectureship, he was also an Associate of the Institute of Chartered Accountants and practiced accounting during his time at Newcastle. Atkinson was also a very keen and able golfer and frequently represented Northumberland in inter-county matches. He was said to be one of the strongest golfers in the north of England and was secretary of the City Golf Club and honorary secretary of the Northumberland Union of Golf Clubs.

In the summer of 1915, he was commissioned into the Durham Light Infantry and served in France where he was wounded in March 1916. On his recovery, he served in France for a second period before being invalided home in November 1917. Once again he recovered his health and was sent back to France in June 1918. On 2 October, he was serving with the 20th Battalion in the lines near Ypres, when his unit came under enemy attack. Atkinson fell while encouraging his men to counter-attack the enemy; he died of his wounds two days later.

Sub-Lieutenant Robert Allen: HMS *Actaeon*, RNVR, 23 or 29 November 1918.

Robert Allen volunteered for naval service shortly after the declaration of war and was commissioned as a Sub-Lieutenant in November of 1914. Initially, he was posted to serve with the Tyne Patrol before being transferred to the Nore Forces (covering the Thames Estuary and adjacent coastline) where he was engaged in mine laying and general patrol work. In the early months of 1918, Allen was either posted or loaned temporarily to the Dover Patrol which operated in the English Channel and off the Belgian coast.

On 23 April, Allen was crewing one of the four motor launches which were to act as guides and support to HMS *Vindictive* during the infamous Zeebrugge Raid.[116] The motor launches came under extremely heavy fire and suffered serious casualties but received great praise for the work that they undertook; such was the impression created by the bravery of the crews of the launches that the commanding officer, Captain Ralph Collins, RN was inducted into the Most Honourable Order of the Bath.

After this costly operation Allen was posted back to the Nore Patrol where he continued to serve until the end of the war. In late November, Sub-Lieutenant Allen unfortunately developed a severe chill while on patrol and this turned to pneumonia. Allen was transferred to RN Hospital Chatham for treatment but died on either the 23 or the 29 November,

Captain Stroud.

aged 31 years-old. In the Roll of Honour of the Royal Grammar School, Robert Allen was described as being 'Kindly, unaffected and straight in every act, Robbie Allen won the love and respect of all who knew of him.'[117] Sub Lieutenant Allen is buried at Newcastle (All Saints) Cemetery.

Captain Henry Clifford Stroud: Royal Flying Corps (formerly Royal Engineers), 7 March 1918.
Henry Clifford Stroud was the son of Professor Henry Stroud who taught at Armstrong College. After leaving the Royal Grammar School, he took a BSc in engineering at Armstrong College before moving on to take a BA at King's College, Cambridge. While at Armstrong he was an enthusiastic member of the Officer Training Corps and a prominent member of many societies, and also he was described as being highly gifted, an athlete, versatile scholar and a lover of music. He was a graduate of the North-East Coast Institution of Engineers & Shipbuilders and had read several papers before the institution and received a number of prizes. In 1912, he was gazetted as a Second Lieutenant in the Territorial Force and when war was declared immediately volunteered for overseas service.

Captain Stroud crash site memorial.

Captain Stroud memorial inscription.

Captain Stroud's grave.

Stroud was posted to France with the 1st Field Company of the (Northumbrian) Royal Engineers. On 8 February 1915, he was severely wounded in both legs and, after several months of treatment in France, was sent home to Armstrong College which was then being used as 1st Northern General Hospital in May. His injuries were so severe that a return to front-line action was deemed impossible and he was subsequently appointed as an instructor in field engineering and bombing. In June 1916, he was promoted to captain but was unhappy with his non-combatant role and instead sought to apply for a commission in the RFC. Stroud proved an able student and quickly gained his wings before being gazetted as a qualified pilot in September.

In Autumn 1917, Captain Stroud was posted to a squadron involved in the air defence of London and became an acknowledged expert flyer and was one of the few who were skilled at night flying (then in its infancy). Serving with 61 Squadron, he took part in attacking many of the raids against southern England. On the night of 7/8 March 1918, a lone raider was reported heading for London in poor weather. Stroud was one of the few pilots qualified to fly in such conditions and took off

*Captain Stroud
Plaque originally
on the memorial
but now at
gravesite.*

from Rochford, Essex in SE5a (B679). At around midnight his aircraft was in collision with a BE12 of 37 Squadron. Stroud and the pilot of the other aircraft were killed. A very-well attended memorial service was subsequently held for Captain Stroud at St Thomas' Church in his home town. The farmer who owned the land where two aircraft crashed erected monuments to both men which still stand. Captain Stroud is buried at St Andrew's Church, Rochford.

Sapper Rupert Victor Bulmer: Royal Engineers,[118] 6 November 1918.
Rupert Victor Bulmer was the son of John and Ada Bulmer of 7 Salisbury Gardens, Jesmond. Bulmer was severely wounded at Ypres and returned to a Newcastle hospital for medical attention. Sadly he died of his injuries in the last week of the war, aged 22 years-old. He is buried at St Nicholas Churchyard and is commemorated by a large monumental headstone.

1st Engineer George Cockburn: Mercantile Marine, 25 August 1918.
Born in Newcastle, George Cockburn was educated at Dame Allan's and Rutherford College. At 40 years-old, he was employed as a marine

engineer. Serving as chief engineer aboard the SS *Willingtonia*, which was sailing from Barry, Wales to Corfu with a cargo hold of coal for the Mediterranean fleet. The *Willingtonia* was owned by the Newcastle-based Ericsson Shipping Company and was a new 3,228-ton steel-hulled cargo ship built in 1918 by the Iron Shipbuilding Co., Newcastle.[119] When the vessel was 13 miles off Maritimo it was torpedoed and sunk by UC-27, a German mine-laying submarine. Four of the crew were lost, including Cockburn. The captain of the ship reported that George Cockburn had lost his life while attempting to save several shipmates. The Admiralty later issues a certificate praising his devotion to duty and he received a special mention in the *London Gazette* of 15 February 1919. He is commemorated on the Tower Hill Memorial; a plaque and also a book of remembrance at the John Knox Presbyterian Church (now Jesmond United Reform Church).

Captain Ralph Broomfield Pritchard, DSO, MC: 12th/13th Battalion, Northumberland Fusiliers, attached to 2nd Battalion, Lincolnshire Regiment, 26 April 1918.

A very brave young officer, Ralph Pritchard was educated at the Royal Grammar School and worked on the staff of the Newcastle upon Tyne Insurance Committee. At the declaration of war, he immediately enlisted, as did many young men, as a private in the 16th Northumberland Fusiliers (1st 'Tyneside Commercials'). His leadership potential was quickly recognized and he was promoted to Second Lieutenant and seconded to the 27th Northumberland Fusiliers (4th 'Tyneside Irish'). By February 1916, he had been promoted to captain. While taking part in the first day of the Somme offensive, he was wounded and when recovered he was posted to the 12th/13th Battalion, Northumberland Fusiliers but immediately attached to the Lincolnshire Regiment.

At the end of 1916, Pritchard was mentioned in dispatches for his work and again just a few months later. For further acts of bravery he was awarded the Military Cross and the Distinguished Service Order and in October 1917, promoted to the rank of acting major. On the disbandment of his battalion he relinquished this rank and became a captain again. On 16 April 1918, during heavy fighting he was seriously wounded and died of his wounds at a casualty clearing station ten days later. After his death he was again mentioned in dispatches.

Second Lieutenant William Alwyn Pritchard: 3rd Battalion, Durham Light Infantry, attached 1st Battalion, Wiltshire Regiment, 26 April 1918.

William Pritchard was the younger brother of Captain Pritchard and he was killed on the same day that his elder brother died. Educated at Royal Grammar School he subsequently entered the insurance industry in Newcastle. He volunteered for service in January 1916 and became a private in the 3rd Northumberland Fusiliers and took part in the fighting on the Somme where was wounded. After being sent home to recover, he returned to the front in December of 1916. He received a commission and was posted to the DLI but attached to the Wiltshire Regiment and involved in heavy fighting throughout March and April 1918. On 26 April, after a German counter-attack Second Lieutenant Pritchard was reported missing. His body was recovered and he is buried in the British Cemetery, Poelcapelle.[120]

Notes

106 *Newcastle Weekly Chronicle*, 12 September 1914.

107 North East War Memorials Project [http://www.newmp.org.uk/detail.php?contentId=9704], accessed 15 January 2014.

108 North East War Memorials Project website [www.newmp.org.uk/detail.php?contentId=9704], accessed 14 January 2014.

109 Barker. Ralph: *The Royal Flying Corps in France: From Bloody April 1917 to Final Victory* (1995), pp. 46.

110 Bowyer. Chaz (ed): *Royal Flying Corps Communiques 1917-1918* (1998), pp. 43.

111 Franks. Norman, Guest. Russell and Bailey. Frank: *Bloody April...Black September* (1995), pp. 76.111 B

112 North East War Memorials Project website [www.newmp.org.uk/detail.php?contentId=9704], accessed 14 January 2014.

113 North East War Memorials Project website [www.newmp.org.uk/detail.php?contentId=9505], accessed 12 November 2013.

114 Account taken from The Wartime Memories Project [http://www.wartimememoriesproject.com/greatwar/allied/view.php?uid=20473], accessed February 2014.

115 Interestingly, both of the ships in which Pittendrigh served before HMS Hussar were sunk. HMS *Drake* was off Ireland in late 1917 and HMS *Sarnia* was torpedoed by U-65 in the Mediterranean on 12 September 1918.

116 For an analysis of this operation see Warner. Philip: *The Zeebrugge Raid* (Pen & Sword, 2008).

117 Royal Grammar School *Book of Remembrance*, taken from North East War Memorials Project website, Ref: J1.19 [www.newmp.org.uk/detail.php?contentId=7777], accessed November 2013.

118 There is some confusion over the regiment to which Bulmer belonged as the grave states his rank as a Sapper in the Royal Engineers while the CWGC website lists him as a Private in the East Yorkshire Regiment.

119 The company had something of a cursed reputation as of the first twenty-five ships it built had sunk or been wrecked. Of its first fifty vessels only three survived a full service life at sea.

120 North East War Memorial Project website [www.newmp.org.uk/detail.php?contentId=9704], accessed 15 January 2014.

Index